BERLITZ®

D0681074

PROVENCE

- A ✓ in the text denotes a highly recommended sight
- A complete A–Z of practical information starts on p.115
- Extensive mapping throughout: on cover flaps and in text

Printed in Switzerland by Weber SA, Bienne.

1st edition (1994/1995)

Although we make every effort to ensure the accuracy of the information in this guide, changes do occur. If you have any new information, suggestions or corrections to contribute, we would like to hear from you. Please write to Berlitz Publishing at the above address.

Text: Giles Allen
Editors: Donald Greig, Sarah Hudson
Photography: Jon Davison
Layout: Suzanna Boyle
Cartography: Visual Image
Thanks to: Catherine Séïté Allen, Vincent Miscopain and Wang
                 Hoa Khoe for their invaluable help and advice in the
                 preparation of this guide.

Cover photographs: (front) Rochefort-en-Valdaine, Drome
                    (back) Chapelle-des-Penitents-Blancs, Les Baux

CONTENTS

Provence and its People

Ask any Frenchman where he wants to live in France, and the chances are that nine times out of ten the answer will be Aix-en-Provence. Ask a non-Frenchman where he views as a paradise on earth, and a disproportionate number of votes will probably be heaped upon one area: Provence.

Why is this tiny corner of France so beloved of the gods, and what more does it offer than other parts of the planet? In short, why is it so irresistibly seductive?

For a start, it was bestowed with a land and nature that must resemble the Garden of Eden – everything not only grows, but also flourishes. The human race realized this very early on: the Greeks arrived from Phocaea (Foça in Turkey) in Asia Minor, and were followed by the Romans, who found much to their taste. Successive generations then simply built on the Gallo-Roman heritage, with a peak in the Middle Ages, the Midi's Golden Age, when Provence set the tone for courtly love and *galanterie* at such places as Forcalquier, Aix, Les Baux and Avignon. Here lie the most important Roman remains in all France, and in the Provençal language and people of today you can feel the Gallo-Roman of nearly 2,000 years ago.

Provence joined France in 1482, with Avignon following in 1791, Nice in 1860, and Tende in 1947. The region's development did not always go hand-in-hand with that of the rest of France. Indeed, particularly in the Middle Ages, its culture, with troubadours and minstrels, and its respect for antiquity, was considered superior to that of northern France. Subsequently, however, er, the language of the region, *Occitan*, lost out to the language of the north, gradually becoming a patois that you occasionally hear spoken in more remote communities.

Who exactly are the Provençaux? Although the people mixed and intermarried with **5**

*E*ndless discussions help to pass the time beneath the shady plane trees in village squares such as at Malaucène.

invaders and settlers, today's inhabitants have a well-defined character. Jovial and generous, optimistic and outgoing, boisterous but sensitive – the Provençal is envied by other Frenchmen simply for his way of being, because, truth to tell, the northern French are too Cartesian, cool and logical to qualify amongst their southern counterparts. Endlessly talking, always joking, the Prov-

ençal's belief is strong that life is there to have fun – and they know how to do just that. As for visitors – they need only show willing to go along with the style of things to be accepted by the Provençaux.

The North-South Divide

It is here the north ends and the south begins. The Midi and northern France are unmistakably different, but indefinably linked by their Frenchness.

From Orange southwards, the strength of the Latin world comes into play, with Provence retaining just that trace of northern rationality making it accessible to all. More strikingly than in other Latin countries, here moderation tempers excess, the arts are appreciated at all levels of society, and food, health, comfort and quality of life, social position and money (in that order) are preoccupations that will concern everyone.

North from Orange, the land may be beautiful and charming, but it isn't quite in the same league. You are told this often, and there's more than a chance that you'll agree.

Recently Peter Mayle's *A Year In Provence* has drawn attention to this region, barely larger than a cabbage patch in world terms, and yet home to all kinds of worlds in itself. The book highlighted the Lubéron in particular, from Cavaillon out east, which to many forms the essence of today's 'regenerated' Provence.

Other diverse areas are also incorporated: the Alpilles, the most alluring of mini-mountain chains; Avignon, the capital, 'reigning' over its territory, the Comtat Venaissin; neighbouring Nîmes, with its superb Roman *maison carrée*, and a touch of aloof dignity; and Arles, more rough-and-ready, but once a Roman capital and spiritual home of Van Gogh, and now enjoying its bullfights. Finally there's Aix-en-Provence, the birthplace of Cézanne and home to France's most popular university, a delightful, civilized city. Small

towns or overgrown villages such as Carpentras or Cavaillon, Roussillon or Gordes each have something special, something distinguishable, and yet could only be Provençal.

No village should be without its boulevard ring (with or without former ramparts), its plane trees, congested traffic, red-tiled roofs, shady squares, gentle fountains, and a church with its wrought-iron belfry. The sharp click of *boules* fills the air, waiters shuffle at outdoor cafés, and old men chat on rickety chairs installed outside their houses, reliving the past in loud, sonorous voices that echo around the squares.

In little hamlets nestling beneath mountains, life continues to follow the same rhythm. Out in the country, in isolated *mas* or farmhouses, even if the surroundings are different, the concerns and topics of conversation have remained the same since time immemorial.

Provençal landscapes vary from the large vineyards of excellent wines (like *Côtes-de-Provence*) to barren gorse- and **8** *maquis*- (scrub) covered hills,

*L*anguorous cats lounge about, while villagers sort out the score of a tranquil game of boules.

where limestone rock gleams under the sun. The valleys and plains are verdant and fertile (more than a fair share of the world's greatest agricultural produce is grown here), while the exposed patches of mountain appear scorched, rocky and rather desolate.

Apart from the flat Rhône delta, Provence is often hilly, or even mountainous as you head towards the Alps. Vineyards stretch to the foot of the Alpilles, while cypresses loom above olive trees and almond groves, and pines provide the shelter for a siesta.

Pétanque and Power Stations

It would be a mistake to think of Provence as nothing but a picturesque backwater full of charming, old-fashioned, garrulous Frenchmen, cigarettes dangling from their mouths, playing *boules* all day. Nuclear power stations and futuristic research laboratories are part and parcel of the modern day Provence – just try the mini-Silicon Valley, Sophia-Antipolis, for size. Furthermore, an increasing number of international firms are moving their headquarters to Provence.

Fashion is up-to-date and cultural activity is also thriving, especially in the summer

months, when each town uses its ancient amphitheatre, cathedral or palace as a magnificent setting for music, theatre and arts festivals. Out of the literary world have come modern writers Pagnol and Giono as well as Daudet and Mistral from the previous generation.

Getting around is no problem, for the motorways are not only practical, but also a scenic pleasure, although parking spaces are as rare as rain in summer in villages barely able to cope with the car invasion.

This human input has, of course, influenced the look of the landscape, but for many the most important pleasure of Provence remains its sensuality. As you drive through the

scrubland (*garrigue*), keep the window down to let in the fragrance of lavender, wild rosemary, thyme and savory, to which local market gardeners also add sage, tarragon and marjoram to make up the famous *herbes de Provence*.

Administratively, Provence-Côte d'Azur forms a single region, governed as a unit from Paris. Each of the multitude of *pays* has its idiosyncracies, however, and amongst Provençaux at least, they matter. The heart of the region is the Avignon-Arles-Aix triangle, but, geographically, is it really so neat and clear? Where does Provence begin and end? Is it where the rooftops change to the red tiles of the Romans? Where cicadas begin to sing? Where the olive trees grow? Where that twangy and pungent accent, so redolent of the south, starts to be heard? Or is it where the *mistral* blows, sometimes infuriatingly? Or where *salade niçoise* and *pissaladière* figure on the menus?

Provence is an ill-defined region that kept on changing throughout history, and which is as big or as small as the speaker wishes. In its broadest sense, it begins with Montélimar and includes Marseille,

*S*traddling the River Gardon, the Pont du Gard stands as one of the civil engineering wonders of the world.

Nice and some of the Côte d'Azur; in its narrower sense, it begins around Orange and finishes with Manosque, Aix-en-Provence, Forcalquier and Sisteron.

Sweet Dictatorship

Binding all regions, however, is that most benevolent of dictators, the sun. Where else can you find this luminosity, the quality of light loved by artists from Cézanne to Van Gogh, and Bonnard to Renoir. It is hardly surprising that Cubism first took shape with Braque's *Paysage de l'Estaque* (1908) beneath a light that accentuates volumes.

However, as Pagnol's *Jean de Florette* and *Manon des Sources* highlight, the glorious sun of Provence brings with it altogether different concerns: rain, or rather the lack of it for the mainly agricultural interior, not to mention the constant threat of forest fires.

But there's no questioning the influence of the elements on Provençal cuisine: full of character, pungent, with herbs and strong-smelling garlic, delicious fruit and varied vegetables. Since everything is organized around the climate, dinner is eaten later than in the north of France, and you will often dine late outside.

Activities are wide-ranging, from hiking around the sweet-smelling countryside to swimming in the Mediterranean, from rafting down the fast-flowing River Verdon to sightseeing at the Pont du Gard – never forgetting that most agreeable of midday pursuits, the Provençal picnic.

We have chosen the most interesting highlights to convey the atmosphere of Provence. You will cross different layers of Provençal life: the Roman towns Orange, Nîmes and Arles; the medieval bastions of Les Baux and Avignon; the essence of Provençal landscape in the mountains of the Lubéron; Aix-en-Provence – that exquisite city chosen by the counts of Provence as their capital; as well as excursions to Haute-Provence.

Bon voyage, bonnes vacances, and above all, bon appétit!

A Brief History

Around the year 600 BC, when the Provence area was inhabited by Ligurians, the Greeks founded and settled Marseille (Massilia), setting up a successful trading station, while the Celts, coming in from the east, were in the process of establishing Gaul.

In 125 BC, the Greeks called in the Romans to help against the roving tribes of motley Celts and Ligurians, who were duly quashed near Aix by the consul Sextius in 122 BC. Sextius proceeded to found a city there, which he named *Aquae Sextiae*. Strategically, the Romans were in need of a direct route to their recently conquered Spanish provinces, and the occasion was too good; they simply helped themselves to a vast region which they called *Provincia Romana*, later corrupted to *Provence*, with its capital, Narbonne.

The Romans took a distinct liking to the place. Indeed, in the words of Pliny, they considered it 'a second Italy', and Caesar wasted no time (59-51 BC) in capturing the whole of Gaul. In the process, he also swallowed up Massilia (Marseille) which, although theoretically allied with Rome, had unfortunately backed Caesar's rival, Pompey, in the Roman Civil War.

After 30 BC, Emperor Augustus set up a first-rate administration, and thanks to the road network across Provence, Italy was linked with Spain via Mont Genèvre, and Arles, on the Rhône, became the most important port in the whole of southern France.

Rome's Indelible Stamp

The effects of four centuries of Roman influence go deep into Provençal consciousness. Towns razed to the ground in Barbarian incursions are still today finding traces of their Roman origins.

Not only was transalpine Gaul generally considered as a delightful place and the first choice for many veteran soldiers to settle, it also served as a rich breadbasket.

Nîmes, taking over the position Marseille had occupied, reached its pinnacle in the 1st century BC. Christianity began to make headway from AD 95, though the first real testimony – an inscription in Arles – dates from AD 254.

The first Provençal monastery was founded on the Ile de Lérins in the 5th century by St Honorat. By the 6th century, the conversion of the people to Christianity was complete, but other problems had arisen in the meantime.

In the 3rd century, Emperor Diocletian had created a new province, Vienne, across the Rhône from the capital, Narbonne. A subdivision in AD 375 made Aix the capital. All in all, the south east of Gaul was better protected from invasion than the rest of the kingdom; indeed, Arles lived its grand era under Constantine in AD 306, later becoming the seat of the religious prefecture in AD 395, taking over from Trier in Germany, which by this time was considered

*R*ome has left its stamp on every vestige and village of Provence, including Nîmes (right) and Vaison-la-Romaine (below).

too close to Barbarian hordes of the east.

By now the Roman empire was beginning to crumble beneath successive invasions and internal problems, and from AD 413, Gaul was trampled underfoot by Saxons, Vandals and Ostrogoths (the Visigoths took Arles in AD 471), until the Franks annexed the land in AD 535.

There are few reliable records about the anarchy which ensued. Charles Martel ('the Hammer'), ruler of the Franks, intervened in AD 736 to quash a rebellion in the area, supported, it would seem, by the Muslims in Spain. Then, just over 30 years after the Frankish conquest in AD 843, Provence fell to Lothair I by the Treaty of Verdun. Under the leadership of Charles, Lothair's son, Provence became a separate entity, initially allied with Burgundy and Lorraine and administered by viscounts and counts. A new threat appeared during the 8th-9th centuries, when Spanish Saracens began to penetrate inland. In AD 884 they set up a virtually unassailable base at La Garde-Freinet above Cannes, forcing many local lords to build perched villages.

Provence Takes Shape

As fate would have it, a providential hero happened to be on the scene at the right time. Guillaume le Libérateur beat back the Saracen forces at La Garde-Freinet, and took the title of marquis in AD 942, thereby inaugurating the first Provençal dynasty, and at the same time marking a new era of prosperity for the region. **15**

The province was effectively independent. Agriculture developed and trade increased, and through the interplay of expedient marriages, Provence passed to the counts of Catalonia (1125-1246). Also at this time the Comté de Vénasque, or Comtat Venaissin, was formed and became papal property (after 1274).

The church started a major expansion campaign, in which much of the building material was taken from structures that had stood for centuries. The **16** construction of Romanesque churches and chapels was also inspired by Roman building techniques. Troubadours wandered from court to court, although each had his own centre. From Marseille came Raimbaud de Vacqueras, later Bishop of Toulouse, while Orange claimed Raimbaud d'Orange. Throughout the area, cultural creativity reached unprecedented heights.

Raimond Bérenger V, particularly, did much to organize and unify the province. After his death in 1245, his daughter Béatrice (or Béatrix) was mar-

*S*tatus symbol: the Palais des Papes in Avignon reveals the popes' ostentatious living style.

ried off in 1246 by the cunning Blanche of Castille to ambitious Charles of Anjou (brother of Louis IX), who became count of Provence. From that day onwards, the destiny of Provence was linked to that of the Angevins and, increasingly, to France. Two years later, Louis IX (St Louis) set out from Aigues-Mortes on the 7th Crusade.

Enter the Popes

In 1309, Pope Clement V (formerly Bertrand de Got, Bishop of Bordeaux), unable to cope with the intense struggles and rivalries between the powerful Roman families, abandoned Rome with his 'court' for Avignon (the Holy See had been given the Comtat Venaissin in 1273).

From a small and provincial backwater, the town suddenly swelled into a very important meeting place for diplomats and pilgrims, holy ecclesiastics and very unholy courtiers, who brought with them a sophisticated way of life.

The popes stayed in Avignon for almost 70 years. In returning to Rome, however, they started the Great Schism (1378-1417), when there were sometimes two, or even three rival popes, each with his own following. The popes in Rome and the two anti-popes in Avignon excommunicated each other with monotonous regularity, and each of the powers in Europe chose their papal champion according to their current interests. The situation continued until 1417, when the Council of Constance deposed the anti-popes.

Good King René

Aix-en-Provence rose to be capital of the counts of Provence. In 1434, René d'Anjou – or Good King René – became count of Provence, and with him began a new era of prosperity. The court, refined and **17**

*J*ust one 'layer' of the town – the fortified medieval Haute-Ville of Vaison-la-Romaine.

sophisticated, came under the influence of this distinguished linguist and mathematician. Troubadours' compositions attained new heights, the arts flourished, and the popular René, himself a keen artist, encouraged the School of Avignon painters.

After René's death, Provence passed to his nephew and heir, Charles III du Maine, who in 1482 bequeathed the entire region, with the exception of the Comtat Venaissin and Savoy, to a distant cousin, Louis XI, King of France. The conditions he attached for Provence's independence were confirmed by the Constitution Provençale in 53 'chapters', which the central government in Paris increasingly ignored as time went on, aided in particular by Richelieu and Louis XIV. The Jews, for instance, protected in the papal territories, were persecuted in France, and many fled or converted to Christianity.

This caused constant friction between Provence and the French government, as well as a number of open rebellions and attempts to secede. Meanwhile, the profound religious problems shaking the whole country took a notably tragic turn in the Midi, where the Reformation made deep inroads, though less so specifically in Provence, where the main problems lay with the heretical Vaudois (named after Pierre Vaudès, who based his creed on the Gospels) from the Lubéron area.

Despite all warnings, they persisted in their beliefs, more or less in line with Protestantism, and resorted on occasions to violence. In 1545, the normally fairly tolerant François I ordered them to be disbanded by force. The result was that 2,000 were killed (hanged, drawn or quartered), and hundreds of others were turned into galley slaves. Orange, belonging to the House of Nassau in the Low Countries, remained an island of Protestantism in Provence.

In 1660, Louis XIV made one of his rare visits outside his royal palace, coming with great pomp to Marseille, then

Plagues and Highwaymen

It sounds like a family parlour game, but in the Middle Ages these were the two major scourges of an already endemically insecure epoch, in which life expectancy plumbed the depths. One of the first plagues, which arrived via Marseille in 1348, wiped out some 30 to 50 percent of the city's population. It returned every 20 years or so for the next century, thinning out the increasingly threadbare numbers.

As if that wasn't enough, hordes of wandering soldiers and brigands made travel a nightmare. Nowhere were they more in evidence than around Avignon. Known as *routiers*, these disbanded soldiers, demobilized after a truce in the Hundred Years' War, often formed independent militia, and would rampage, loot and torture at will. Their attacks were particularly virulent in 1357-58, and the popes were forced to buy them off with pardons and ever-greater sums of money. Towns had to fortify their ramparts and take in hordes of unwanted refugees, and in 1377 one of the reasons for Pope Gregory XI's return to Rome was that he could no longer pay out the exorbitant sums demanded.

emerging as an increasingly important trading port. His objective was to win over the opposition and anchor the city on his side. However, his long-term plans had to be scrapped when, 80 years later, a particularly bad plague swept through the city, leaving a death toll of 38,000, half the population. The toll in all Provence was over 100,000.

Gradually the province did grow, however. The principality of Orange, which had belonged to the Nassau family, fell to France by the Treaty of Utrecht in 1713. In 1791, as the Revolution gathered momentum, the Comtat Venaissin and Avignon, both papal territories, joined France.

Revolution for a Song

On the whole, Provence greeted the Revolution with something like relief. In 1792, some

*T*he village church at Gordes – just one attraction of this much photographed perched village.

500 Marseille soldiers sang their way to Paris, chanting the previously unknown *Song for the Army of the Rhine*, and rousing the massed crowds as they went. In Paris they took part in the insurrection of 10 August, and in their honour, the song came to be known as *La Marseillaise*, the French national anthem of today, despite its Rhineland origins.

Provence was subsequently divided administratively into three separate *départements*: Bouches-du-Rhône, Var, and Basses Alpes, to which the Vaucluse, including the ex-papal territories, was added the following year. The taking of Nice by the revolutionary armies around one year later, though outside the Provence area, added a new *département*, that of the Alpes-Maritimes. It actually reverted to Savoy following Napoleon's defeat, only to return once and for all to France in 1860 in payment for French help given to Italy against Austria.

In most parts of Provence, and in Marseille, Napoleon's departure was welcomed, the **21** revolutionary excesses, executions, and anticlerical violence having resulted in sympathy for the cause to evaporate.

The 19th century was relatively uneventful. Industrialization arrived gradually but inexorably, changing local traditions and customs forever. During the troubles at the start of the Second Republic (1848-51), many Provençaux showed themselves to be ardent Republicans. Meanwhile, Marseille grew in size dramatically, as almost all trade with French Magreb (Algeria, Tunisia and Morocco) passed through the city, and its transformation industries also prospered. Waves of refugees and immigrants came and, mainly, stayed, including Algerians, Armenians, Italians and Spaniards.

Keeping Roots

In the face of these rapid and radical changes was something of a reaction. Southerners in general, and Provençaux in particular, felt that their language and culture were held in contempt by northerners, who considered *Occitan* a 'mere' patois, even going so far as to punish children who spoke it at school.

It was at this time that the *Félibrige*, a regional organization working against the abandonment of local culture and language in favour of French, was (appropriately so) born at a copious lunch on 21 May 1854. Its aim was to settle the argument over the spelling of Provençal once and for all, and to restore it as a language in its own right. Even if they failed to put a stop to the progress of French, which had become absolutely necessary for social advancement, this movement did at least help to make the region as a whole, and in particular Marseille, more aware of its *Occitan* roots.

At the outbreak of World War I, Marseille had 500,000 inhabitants, and in competition with Aix, beat it hands down. Aix languished through most of the l9th century as a provincial, slightly musty, if distinguished, backwater, with a population numbering a mere 25,000. At around this time, artists such as Cézanne (in Aix) and Van Gogh (in Arles and Saint-Rémy) started to appreciate the arid beauty of the Provençal landscape and to capture its spirit on canvas. This new departure, using the landscapes of the south – initially the coast, later inland – as subject matters in their own right, soon made an impression. Dufy, Braque, Matisse, Signac, Derain, not to mention Picasso, Vasarely, de Staël,

---

Oc or Oïl?

Derived directly from Latin, Provençal was established with a firm linguistic base in the 4th century. By the 9th century it had spread throughout the Midi (the South of France), thanks largely to wandering troubadours (strolling minstrels) between Nice in the east and Aquitaine in the west. Their poetry, courtly tales and sophisticated imagery were to influence the whole course of European literature.

Provençal is also known as *Occitan*, meaning 'language of Oc', with *Oc* meaning 'yes', just as *oïl* does in the language of northern France (the language that eventually became 'correct' French – hence '*oui*'). In the 15th century, *Occitan* began to break down into a number of more localized dialects. In 1539, when François I decreed that French would be the sole language of administration, he dealt a fatal blow to *Occitan*. Nonetheless, there has been a partial recovery since the foundation in 1854 of the *Félibrige*, a literary school in which Joseph Roumanille and, to a greater extent, author Frédéric Mistral (Nobel Prize winner in 1904), played a big part.

You may come across older people speaking Provençal in out-of-the-way villages, though the numbers are dwindling. Day-to-day French spoken by a Provençal is full of generic terms such as *un pitchoun* (a child), *le cagnard* (the sun), *Boudiou!* (good heavens!), and most common of all, *peuchère!* (good grief!).

*A*griculture, including wine-growing, is as important to the Provençal economy as tourism.

and Masson, all found the Mediterranean landscapes a source of immense inspiration. (We are now rewarded with their colourful works, which have gone on in turn to inspire many artists since.)

The south of France was relatively lightly affected by World War I (though, like the rest of France, it lost many of its men). Occupation by Italy came with World War II, followed in 1942-43 by the same

from the Germans. Marseille's old quarters were largely destroyed in January 1943 whilst the Nazis rapidly built up defences in the area and planted an infinity of minefields. Even this failed to stop the Allies under General Patch who landed at Saint Raphaël in August 1944. Within a fortnight, Provence was liberated. Once it had recuperated two tiny pockets (Tende and La Brigue) from Italy, it again returned to the frontiers of some 2,000 years ago as the *Provincia Romana*.

Since those heady days, Provence has steadily built up its industry and, in particular, its flourishing tourist infrastructure, which now copes with millions of visitors each year. Not surprisingly, this is one of the province's trump economic cards, although not its only one – agriculture and technology count just as much.

The area's natural diversity offers the visitor much to see and do, while its history reveals the worlds of Rome, the Middle Ages, the present and the past, living in harmony beneath balmy, reliable skies.

24

Where to Go

Most visitors approach Provence from the north, where the efficient road network puts everything within easy reach. The first glimpses of the area are, in some parts, unexpectedly mountainous.

Gateway to Provence

Provence vegetation starts to change at Valence. The pretty fields and orchards give way to red poppy fields and purple lavender, cypresses and *garrigue*, vineyards and russet villages, and the sun gets ever stronger. Just past Montélimar, the capital of nougat, Provence beckons.

ORANGE

The grand and ancient monuments of this once prosperous Roman trading centre strike a delightfully incongruous note in the Provençal backwater of today. The town fell by inheritance to the Dutch family of Orange-Nassau in 1530, who, though proud of their 'French' possession, nevertheless dismantled many impressive Roman buildings and temples to build ramparts. These were in turn demolished when Louis XIV, at war with the Netherlands, stormed the town.

Enter the town from the north at the great, three-arched **Arc de Triomphe**. Built during 21 BC (but since restored), it stands on a traffic island across the old N7, which here follows the route of the ancient Via Agrippa. Friezes of naval equipment and fighting soldiers on the north side depict Octavius Caesar's victory over Antony and Cleopatra at the Battle of Actium in 31 BC.

Orange's other great Roman monument, the **Théâtre antique**, is on the south side of town. Historians regard this as the finest and best preserved of the surviving theatres of the Roman Empire. It is unique for its towering, scenic wall, still standing, with a statue of Augustus to greet you. Originally, 7,000 spectators came

Orange's Arc de Triomphe at the entrance to town is the real gateway to Provence.

here from all over Provence to watch a circus, Greek tragedy, Latin comedy or lottery draw. It still provides a wonderful stage for opera and symphony concerts at the July *Chorégies d'Orange* festival (see p.101), first held in 1869 and staged annually since 1902.

The situation of the *théâtre*, nestling within the Colline Saint-Eutrope, enhances its inherent beauty. Louis XIV considered it 'the most beautiful wall in my kingdom'. There is a good view of the surroundings from the top.

VAISON-LA-ROMAINE

A pretty drive 30km (19 miles) north east of Orange along the D975 brings you to the site of one of the most important towns of Roman Provence, excavated to the north of Vaison's modern quarters. These ruins lie right in the middle of town, as much part of things today as they have been for 2,000 years.

Note in particular the **Maison des Messii**, a luxurious villa with fine mosaics; the **Portique de Pompéi**, a kind of public walkway; and the **Théâtre** (lst-3rd century AD), with a *hypocœnia* for the props and colonnade on the upper floor (the only theatre in all Provence to have kept it).

To fully understand the layout of the ancient town, visit the **museum** on Puymin hill. It houses superb marble sculptures from the 2nd century AD, notably those of Venus, the Emperor Hadrian, and his wife

Sabina. Towards the cathedral, in the area by the post office, excavations have unearthed a basilica and two houses.

After visiting the town, do not forget the interesting 11th-12th century Romanesque **cathedral Notre-Dame-de-Nazareth**. The town as a whole makes a delightful stop, despite damage inflicted on the lower (Gallo-Roman) section by torrential rains in autumn 1992. Less affected were the medieval houses of charming **Haute-Ville**, overlooking the Ouvèze, which is entered by a fortified gate. Look out for the house of the rue des Fours, and the Quartier de la Juiverie.

A **Roman bridge** (1st century) with a 17m (55ft), single-span arch links the two parts of town. Across the river to the east lies the strangely haunting Mont Ventoux, while to the west are the *Côtes-du-Rhône* wine villages – not forgetting lovely Carpentras. First, however, we head northward.

The Essentials

In a rush? Here are the principal Provence highlights:

ARLES: Provence's Rome.

AVIGNON: Papal palaces and festivals.

THE ALPILLES: sun, scents and solitude in the *garrigue*.

AIX-EN-PROVENCE: culture with cheer.

LES BAUX-DE-PROVENCE: medieval city in a moonscape.

CARPENTRAS: Provence in a nutshell.

GORDES/SÉNANQUE: Vasarely and village, Cistercian abbey.

THE LUBÉRON: wild mountain chain with villages of character.

MARSEILLE: for fun and shopping.

MONT VENTOUX: more a monument than a mountain.

NIMES: animation and stately dignity.

NORTH OF VAISON-LA-ROMAINE

A scenic drive from Vaison takes you through Tulette and Visan, typical wine villages, to **Valréas**, another town of the Comtat Venaissin, which is surrounded by a protective boulevard. The **Hôtel de Ville** (town hall) is in the former Hôtel de Simiane, which once belonged to the granddaughter of Madame de Sévigné, that ubiquitous and genial woman of letters. It is a majestic, early 18th-century palace with Gothic influences, painted ceilings, splendid furniture and paintings, and a papal bull.

The **church** is interesting as a typically Provençal Romanesque building (in particular the 12th-century porch). Some fine 16th-century paintings inside include a *Circumcision*.

Next, continue west to **Grignan**, for the classical château which belonged to Mme de Sévigné herself. From its hilltop site, the view is splendid – if the *mistral* wind isn't blowing too strongly. Alternatively, head eastwards for **Vinsobres**,

Nyons (famous for its olives), Venterol, and **St-Pantaléon-les-Vignes**, with its particularly sophisticated wines.

WEST OF VAISON

Séguret, at the top of a hill, is a popular spot (leave the car at the entrance to the village). The ruined castle, steep, narrow streets and ancient houses give the village a tremendous appeal. It also enjoys a superb view over the jagged Dentelles (literally 'lace') de Montmirail, across the plain of the Comtat Venaissin and towards the Massif Central.

The fruity red **Gigondas** wine (considered to be among the best *Côtes-du-Rhônes*) is excellent with *terrines,* game, poultry, and cheese, and is most often drunk young. To the north of the picturesque village, which is as an excellent departure point for walks through the hills, rise the gleaming white mountains, the **Dentelles de Montmirail**, whose curious, jagged shape is unmistakable. Rising to 734m (2,407ft), the rocky peaks are silhouetted against the sky, as the last gasp of Mont Ventoux before it tumbles towards the Rhône. **Vacqueyras**, Montmirail and **Beaumes de Venise** all cluster round the foothills and produce some excellent wines (in particular *Muscat* from Beaumes).

MONT VENTOUX

Leaving Vaison-la-Romaine, moody **Mont Ventoux** looms ever larger. The mountain derives its name from the high winds that buffet its 1,909m (6,263ft) peak (one pass is known as the *Col des Tempêtes* – 'Storm Pass'). The top can be reached on the D974, by way of lavender fields and meadows dotted with larch and cedar of Lebanon, from the attractive village of **Malaucène**, with its 16th-century

Nyons, an old Roman town at the foot of the Alps, is the capital of olive-growing.

clock-tower. On top of the hillock in the village stand the remains of a small château and a square belfry. In summer, a first-rate arts and theatre festival is held here.

It is also popular hiking and biking country, but take it easy – British cyclist Tom Simpson met with a tragic end on the mountain during the *Tour de France* of 1967.

Comtat Venaissin

Small it may have been, but up until the French Revolution the popes had their own bit of French territory – the Comtat Venaissin. It was bounded by the Rhône, the Durance, and Mont Ventoux, and it covered much of the *département* today called the Vaucluse, including Apt, Orange, Carpentras, Cavaillon, and Avignon, as well as Vénasque, after which it was named (*Comtat* is Provençal for *comté*, or county).

It was given to the popes in 1320, following a treaty which officially endorsed the suppression of the Albigensian heresy (*la guerre des Albigeois*), but which – reading between the lines – was more influenced by the defeat of the pro-Cathar counts of Toulouse.

During its spell as papal capital, Carpentras enjoyed great prosperity – at least while the popes were in Avignon. It outgrew its original walls, at which point a new set (including the Porte d'Orange) was built. Pope Clement V actually called the Comtat Venaissin 'the garden of my delights', and Carpentras enjoyed a time of outrageous favouritism.

When the popes returned to Rome in the early 15th century, the Comtat became a neglected, almost forgotten possession. It finally reverted to France after the Revolution in 1791, when all Church possessions were summarily 'reclaimed'. The economic situation improved enormously in the 19th century when a canal was built, and from being poor and inhospitable, the region became one of the gardens of France.

Have a rest at the waterfall and café beyond the octagonal, domed **Chapelle Notre-Dame du Groseau**, before starting the climb to the Observatory and the spectacular **view** of the surrounding Provençal countryside. You stand precisely at the point where the snowy Alps of the Dauphiné meet the more clement regions of the south (in winter, there's skiing). It may be isolated and barren up here, but look down the other side of Mont Ventoux at the delights that await. You can see all the way from the Alps to Marseille, even to the Cévennes and – so they say – the Pyrenees (Mont Canigou).

As you head down, through enchanting **Bédoin** (look in the church for the 14 panels attributed to Mignard), notice the rapid change in vegetation: bees flourish (providing excellent honey), lavender jumps to life in spring, and precious truffles prosper. You can then head down to flower-bedecked **Le Barroux**, with its towering Renaissance (restored) château, or delightful **Caromb** in the plain. Note, however, that in this mountainous part, roads are few and narrow.

For more of the same type of scenery, take the D164 to **Sault**, famous for its lavender fields. From its lofty position at 765m (2,509ft), it looks out over Mont Ventoux. Carry on through **Monieux**, with its medieval tower and Romanesque houses, and then to the lovely **Gorges de la Nesque** (lay-bys are scarce).

CARPENTRAS

In its heyday, from 1320 until the French Revolution, **Carpentras** was capital of the Comtat Venaissin, (the popes' territories). From its Roman origins it has kept a **triumphal arch**, where the grand trophies of war demonstrate the preoccupations of the time.

The only part of the walls which remains is the 14th-century **Porte d'Orange**, but you can sense the rampart-boulevards running round the city. Indeed it's a good idea to drive round the boulevards (particularly for the colourful Friday market), although you should **31**

Behind major arteries lie the charming back streets – such as those at Carpentras.

avoid driving into the centre, with its confusing labyrinth of narrow winding streets. Stroll through the smart shops and absorb the atmosphere of this compact town on foot.

Right in the centre lies the former **cathedral of Saint-Siffrein**, which was begun as early as 1404 by the Bishop of Arles, who later became Pope Benoît XIII of Avignon. Enter via the flamboyant Gothic portal of the **Porte Juive**, so **32** called because it was formerly

reserved for Jews who had just converted to Christianity. In the former bishopric the **Palais de Justice** has retained its 17th-century decoration, while the 18th-century **Hôtel-Dieu** still has its pharmacy, with faience jars, tubes and glasses.

The most unusual monument Carpentras has to offer is also France's oldest **synagogue**. In the papal territories the Jews found a refuge where they enjoyed a relatively privileged status. The sumptuous synagogue was rebuilt in 1741 in place of an older building dating from 1367, and was erected by a community of only 750 families.

Outside the town, you will want to visit **Vénasque**, from where the Comtat Venaissin got its original name. It was capital of the enclave between the 6th and the end of the 10th centuries, a long time before

Carpentras. Occupying a magnificent position on a promontory, with large oaks providing welcome shade, it incorporates the 7th-century Merovingian **baptistery**, which amazingly still features its original Corinthian columns.

Nearby, the town of **Pernes-les-Fontaines** also had a time as capital of the Comtat (from AD 968-1320), and today is the centre of a fruit-growing area, the produce of which – grapes, cherries and melons – can be found at the market on the **Cours de la République**.

The town owes its name to its numerous fountains (32 in total), the most striking being the **Fontaine du Cormoran**. The 13th-century **Tour Ferrande** has some interesting **frescoes** from around 1275, showing various unidentified knights and notables as well as several versions of the *Virgin and Child*. The Roman **bridge** straddles the River Nesque on the edge of the town, separating the **Porte Notre-Dame** (1548) and a charming, small part-Romanesque church, the Église Notre-Dame.

Western Provence

With the Rhône as their lifeline, the Romans developed a brilliant network of communications and prestigious cities on both sides of the river.

Take the trip across the Rhône to some of the most impressive sights in France.

We begin at the Pont du Gard, one of the grandest feats of engineering, which carried a city's water supply up a gentle incline in a way that even today leaves us amazed at the Romans' technical prowess.

PONT DU GARD

Take the A9 *autoroute* going south west from Orange to the Fournès-Remoulins exit, and follow the D981 to the parking lot in front of the bridge.

In the Gardon Valley's wonderful natural setting of forest and river, this gigantic, 2,000-year-old **aqueduct** (historians estimate it was constructed around AD 19) is the most impressive of all Roman **33** monuments preserved from ancient Gaul. Parts of the original works, which were used to carry spring water from near Uzès to Nîmes (a distance of 35km/22 miles), have survived, though the system as a whole fell into disuse around

Including a barrage of sieges, the Pont du Gard has resisted assaults for over 2,000 years.

the 8th century. The stunning aqueduct stands 49m (160ft) above the river, and an easy marked path leads to the top.

Built of huge granite blocks joined without mortar, this highly functional construction is in total harmony with its landscape. It has survived remarkably intact, despite attempts made at various times to use some of the masonry for building elsewhere. The roof walkway is 275m (902ft) long, and not too difficult to negotiate. The best view of it is from the riverbank near the Château Saint-Privat. A visit here will take about an hour.

NÎMES

Nîmes was given as a gift by Emperor Augustus to the veterans of his victorious battle against Antony and Cleopatra in Egypt, which is commemorated to this day by the chained crocodile of the Nile in the Nîmes coat-of-arms.

The grand **amphitheatre** (*arènes*) was built for gladiator battles, and later used for enforced combat between lions

---

Beastly Men

Whatever one's views on bullfighting today, even more gory things happened in the same rings in Roman times.

In the amphitheatre, all non-Romans condemned to death were either executed or abandoned to wild animals for a public contest. Most of the time, however, the bullring was used for 'entertainment' combats, often offered to the people as a kind of electoral propaganda by high-ranking officials.

At the event, officials would sit in the lower boxes, behind the protective wall, with lesser figures behind them, up to the top tiers occupied by slaves. The smell of the wild beasts was smothered by perfume, and slaves sprayed scent over the officials to keep them fresh, while the sand was covered with red chalk, so that the blood would be less conspicuous.

Specially trained, the gladiators, often slaves, but sometimes just pugnacious Gauls, had little alternative but to win or be killed. The winner would be freed, while the loser could beg for mercy from the president, who, basing his decision on public opinion, would give either a 'thumbs up' or 'thumbs down'. If grace was refused, the victor had to put an end to the loser's suffering, and the deceased would be dragged out by his feet.

---

and Christians. In its heyday, it held 21,000 spectators. Having served as a fortress against the invading Visigoths in the 5th century, and then as a communal residence for the poor in the Middle Ages, it has now resumed the ancient bloody tradition with summer bullfights – visit the exhibition at the **Musée du Vieux Nîmes**.

The more peaceful, Greek-style temple known as the **Maison Carrée** is an elegant monument from the same era (1st century BC), which is noted for the finely sculpted Corinthian capitals on its columns. Like several Roman remains in the Marseille area, Greek influence is superimposed on Roman. After a varied history **35** as town hall, residence, stable and church, it was saved from a project of Louis XIV's minister, Colbert, to move it stone by stone to Versailles. Today it houses the small but interesting **Musée des Antiques**, which covers Roman sculpture and mosaics.

The **Jardin de la Fontaine** is a tree-shaded, 18th-century park at the north-west edge of town on the slopes of Mont Cavalier. Offering respite from the heat, as well as a good **view** of the surrounding Cévennes mountains, the park is built round the spring of Nemausus, which gave the town its name.

As for the Roman **Tour Magne**, it probably dates from the end of the 1st century BC, though what it served as remains a mystery. In any case, it seems to have shrunk by some 10m (33ft), due to the peculiar exploits in 1601 of a madcap gardener, who was convinced that treasure was buried here; in his haste he undermined the foundations by digging below them. Needless to say, he died ruined, still a gardener.

Nîmes has retained a quiet dignity, though it is very much a town of the south. (At bullfight time, excitement reaches a frenzy.) In the old town, **Rue de l'Aspic**, **Rue des Marchands**, and **Rue Dorée**, all with 16th-17th century *hôtels*, deserve investigation, and lead up to the much-restored **cathedral of Notre-Dame**.

Finally, gourmets rave over the local *olives confites* and the *brandade de morue*; it would be a pity not to try them.

SAINT-GILLES

Surrounded by orchards, on the fringe of the Camargue, **Saint-Gilles** stands at a crossroads on an important route taken by pilgrims to Santiago de Compostela. Though now a modest town, it is home to what many consider to be, along with Saint-Trophime in Arles, the greatest work of Provençal Romanesque architecture still visible.

Little is left of the monastery, built in 1200 to house the pilgrims, the Wars of Religion having taken their toll.

What do remain, however, are three glorious **portals** in the west front and the crypt with the tomb of St Gilles. Some enthuse about the profusion of beasts of fable on the frieze, as well as the symbols, directly inherited from the Romans; others prefer the extraordinary religious scenes at the base of the central portal, such as *The Last Supper* or *Cain and Abel*. The **Vis de Saint-Gilles** (spiral staircase), built about 1150 in the destroyed north tower, gives some idea of the original importance of the whole.

*T*he symbol of Nîmes (above) and St Gilles' Romanesque crypt, share a distant common ancestry.

Avignon and the Heart of Provence

AVIGNON

The City of the Popes is a businesslike, regional capital, home to 180,000. It is also a proud, national cultural centre, host of one of Europe's greatest arts festivals, with over 300 shows of all kinds between mid-July and mid-August, and a lively, cheerful town full of art galleries, cafés and fashionable shops. The whole is protected from the *mistral* by fine old ramparts.

Opulence and luxury have disappeared from the **Palais des Papes**, but you will still get an idea of the grandeur and above all the embattled situation of these maverick popes, entrenched behind the ramparts of a feudal fortress. Enter on the west through the Porte des Champeaux and join the guided tour across the Grande Cour (now transformed into an open-air theatre for the summer festival) to the **Palais**

vieux. Its formidable design reflects the pious austerity of its builder, Benedict XII.

East of Benedict's cloister is the **consistory**, where the pope met with, and appointed, his cardinals; today it is decorated with the superb **frescoes** of Simone Martini, brought from the porch of Notre-Dame-des-Doms cathedral. Other frescoes, by Matteo Giovannetti, Martini's pupil, can be found in the Chapelle Saint-Jean, the Chapelle Saint-Martial, and in Clément VI's more decorative **Palais nouveau**, where Old Testament prophets adorn the superb ceiling of the Grand Audience Hall.

Beyond the much-remodelled cathedral is the pleasant garden of the **Rocher des Doms**, extending to the outer ramparts and offering the best view of the **Pont d'Avignon** (more properly the Pont Saint-Bénézet), which is broken off halfway across the Rhône.

Built in 1185 in an L-shape (to resist the swirling current), only four spans of the original 23 survived the ice floes and floods of 1670. The bridge has been immortalized in the old song *Sur le pont d'Avignon* (the dancing was in fact *under* the bridge, on a little island, rather than *on* it). In the gardens, look out for the sundial where your own shadow tells the time.

The **Petit Palais** (north end of the Place du Palais), houses a superb collection of Italian paintings from the 13th-16th centuries, which includes several major works by Taddeo Gaddi, Veneziano and Botti-

celli, and Carpaccio's masterpiece, *Holy Conversation*.

At the centre of the bustling, modern town is the airy **Place de l'Horloge**, surrounded by cafés and a pedestrian zone of smart shops along the Rue des Marchands. At the far end is the Place Jérusalem, with its old synagogue.

For a walk through the **old town**, start at the 14th-century **Église Saint-Didier**, with its excruciating altar sculpture, *Jesus Carrying the Cross*, by

---

Popes, Pro and Anti

In 1309, when Pope Clement V moved the Holy See from Rome to Avignon, he stirred up a mini-revolution. Yet seven popes, all French, made their home beside the Rhône, and, like Rome, Avignon became a city of pomp and intrigue. It attracted great Italian artists, such as the poet Petrarch and the Sienese painter Simone Martini, but was soon decried as 'an unholy Babylon' of gaudy luxury and vicious riff-raff. Petrarch himself was all in favour of a return to Rome, which eventually took place when the pious mystic, Catherine of Siena, brought Pope Gregory XI back in 1377.

In 1378, power struggles caused the Great (Western) Schism, in which antipopes set themselves up in Avignon again for a further 40 years, until the Schism ended with their deposition in 1417. The squabbling returned once and for all to Rome, but Avignon remained part of the papal lands in Provence until the French Revolution.

the Dalmatian artist Francesco Laurana. The Rue du Roi-René heads past handsome 17th- and 18th-century houses, while on cobblestoned **Rue des Teinturiers**, you can see where the dyers used to work paddlewheels for their Indian-style cloth, at a spot where the little River Sorgue emerges from underground.

The **Musée Calvet** is comfortably housed in a superb, 18th-century hôtel, in which the **Salle de ferronnerie** (ironwork collection) displays over 6,000 items, from door knockers to shop signs. The Avignon

Not much to dance on, but a lot to be proud of: Avignon's ramparts and Pont St-Bénézet.

School of primitive painters, which flourished between the 14th and 16th centuries, precedes a veritable panorama of French art from the 16th to the 20th centuries, in which virtually every major French artist is represented.

During the summer festival, when the city functions more or less 24 hours a day, head for

Place de l'Horloge and Place du Palais, where you will be transported back to the Middle Ages, complete with troubadours, improvised shows, conjurers, magicians, hawkers and fortune-tellers.

VILLENEUVE-LÈS-AVIGNON

Hop over the Rhône to **Villeneuve-lès-Avignon**, both for superb views of Avignon and the sumptuous abbey **gardens** around the Chapelle Notre-Dame-de-Belvézet. Here we are in former France, or Languedoc to be precise – the historical frontier runs along the Rhône. The cardinals had their country houses in Villeneuve, but were only visitors.

Jean the Good of France constructed **Fort Saint-André** on Mont Andaon from 1362 to 1368 as a hint to the Pope not to go too far, and to keep an eye on him across the river. A walk around the ramparts is beautiful and invigorating.

The **charterhouse** (founded in 1356) appears to be both huge and bare, but the **tomb** (part marble, part local Pernes stone) of Innocent VI, founder of the charterhouse, is admirable. Many of the charterhouse's artistic treasures are displayed in the **museum** of the Hôtel du Luxembourg, the highlight being the 1453-54 *Couronnement de la Vierge* (Crowning of the Virgin) by Enguerrand Quarton, one of the great names of the School of Avignon painters.

Before you leave, visit the 1320 **Église Notre-Dame** for its exquisite 17th-century marble **altarpiece**.

CHÂTEAUNEUF-DU-PAPE

By 1360-61, *Châteauneuf-du-Pape* wines were being favoured by the discerning popes. Alphonse Daudet called the label 'the king of wines and the wine of kings', and there is no doubt that it is among the greatest of the *Côtes-du-Rhônes*. It is also one of the strongest, minimum 12.5 percent, due at least in part to the tremendous heat reflected by the white stony soil.

41

This was the private vineyard of the Pope, around his summer residence, 17km (11 miles) north of Avignon. That nothing now remains of the château but a **tower** is again due to the Wars of Religion and, more recently, the Nazis, who blew up the dungeon. From the top, there is a magnificent **view** towards Avignon and the Alpilles.

LES BAUX-DE-PROVENCE

The astounding natural location of this medieval citadel, a single massive outcrop of rock cut adrift from the Alpilles, exerts a unique grip on the imagination. It may be just 19km (12 miles) from Arles, but it feels like another universe. (Dante – so it is said – drew

his inspiration for hell from Les Baux.) More certain is the fact that the village lent its name to bauxite, which was discovered here in 1822.

In high season, the village surrounding the old **fortress** becomes unbearably crowded, but a visit in early spring, autumn or, best of all, on a crisp winter's day, makes for a rare and treasured moment.

The barons of Les Baux put the star of the Nativity on their coat-of-arms, claiming to be descendants of Balthazar, lord of the treasury among the Three Wise Men. It was with the same brazen pride that they ruled 79 towns of medieval Provence, and their impregnable redoubt became a centre of courtly love, much prized by travelling troubadours. For centuries they defied the papal authority in Avignon as well as the kings of France, offering refuge to rebellious Protestants during the Wars of Religion until Louis XIII ordered the destruction of the fortress in 1632 – and made the residents pay the costs.

Today the **village** of Les Baux is an attractive mixture of boutiques and galleries set in medieval and Renaissance houses, many with delightful gardens. Look at **Rue du Trencat** and the effects of the

Craggy and lunar, Les Baux-de-Provence's medieval fortress blends into the rocky landscape. **43**

elements on the rock, and also at the endearing **Place Saint-Vincent**. The most famous Provençal mass at Christmas, complete with shepherds, is in the **Église Saint-Vincent**.

The demolition of the citadel was clearly a half-hearted job, as you can see when you stroll through the **Ville morte** (Dead City). The ramparts, castle walls and ruined chapels each reveal their own startling view over sheer ravines to the surrounding mountains, from where the winds gust around the village.

Nearby, visit the original **Cathédrale d'images**, where a quite stunning show is staged using 40 projectors with the walls of a former limestone quarry acting as a screen. The theme is different each year.

SAINT-RÉMY-DE-PROVENCE

The jagged peaks of the Alpilles mark the end of the great Alpine chain that sweeps in a 1,200km (750-mile) arc from Vienna. If you're tempted to hike or bike around the valleys, drive on to the charming town of **Saint-Rémy-de-Provence**, in which the *syndicat d'initiative* provides detailed routes and information on bike hire, as well as 'Van Gogh itineraries'. Have a look at the old **church** and nip into the **Hôtel de Sade** to see Roman exhibits collected from excavations at Glanum.

Don't forget the **Musée des Alpilles**, either, a pleasant little museum in a delightful 16th-century house, the Hôtel Mistral de Mondragon.

Glanum is 1 mile (1.5km) outside Saint-Rémy, in the foothills of the Alpilles, on the Roman road between Arles and Milan. Originally a Greek settlement (called Glanon), it was inhabited, like Marseille, by Phocaean Greeks, until Caesar's brutal arrival on the scene in 49 BC, when it was rapidly romanized. It constitutes an excellent picture of a complete Roman town, much influenced by Greek architecture, but in ruins since its destruction in the 3rd century AD by the Germanic hordes. You could learn more about Roman

44

After a bicycle tour around Saint-Rémy-de-Provence, stock up on provisions at one of the town's charming stores.

life here than from many of the bigger sites.

Particularly well-preserved are two monuments known as the *Antiques*: the **mausoleum**, which has survived the centuries looking incredibly fresh, and the **municipal arch**, probably the oldest in Provence, dating from the early years of Augustus (around 40 BC). The beautiful, deep and regular lacunars round the arch inside have hardly suffered.

Just back from the ruins lies the former, serenely beautiful **monastery and cloister of Saint-Paul-de-Mausole**. Here at the psychiatric clinic, Van Gogh was interned between 1889 and 1890, painting some of his most tormented works. **45**

Daudet's famous windmill – a popular testimony to times past – and to the power of legend.

landscapes of Greece, while on the lower slopes, cypresses jostle for position with almond and olive trees.

Beyond Les Baux, the main town to speak of in the Alpilles is **Eygalières** – an overgrown village frequented more today by those on holiday than shepherds. White stone houses and the rocky *garrigue* meld beneath the sun to the extent that it becomes difficult to tell which is which. The village road climbs to the ruined dungeon at the peak of the hill. Just outside the village, make one of those small but delightful halts in Provence, for the minute, 12th-century **chapelle Saint-Sixte**.

A hike through the Alpilles is one of the most enjoyable day excursions you can imagine. Set off from Les Baux, and include Glanum and Saint-Rémy; **Maussane**, famous for

 THE ALPILLES

The **Alpilles** are tiny, a mere bump compared to the mighty Alps to which they are very tenuously attached. Just 25km (15 miles) in length, a few kilometres across, and consisting mostly of barren *garrigue*, they ascend to a short 400m (1,312ft). Yet this is a much loved mountain range, a place where heady scents embalm the air, bewitching the visitor with the sheer *joie-de-vivre* of Provence. The tops of the hills are reminiscent of the arid its olive oil; Eygalières, for a picnic lunch; **Orgon**, for its lovely 14th-century chapel; Eyguières; then on to the picturesque ruins of Castelas de Roquemartine. Take the D25 west to Mas-de-Montfort and head back towards Les Baux.

Alternatively, head in the other direction from Les Baux,

Petrarch – Love at First Sight

Who hasn't heard of Petrarch, yet who knows, beyond his platonic love for Laura, what he actually did? He tells us that his parents were from Florence, but he was born in Arezzo in 1304. At the age of nine, he came with them to Avignon, 'that disgusting city', the 'sewer', as he later called it, where 'the Roman Pontiff holds and has long held the Church of Christ in shameful exile.'

A poet and a humanist, he seems to have travelled a good deal when young, studying law for four years in Montpellier and for three years in Bologna. He returned to Avignon in 1326, and in 1327 fell in love with Laura (possibly Laure de Noves, married in 1325 to Hugo de Sade), a young woman he saw at matins in St Clare Church in Avignon (since disappeared). Most of his poems of the *Canzoniere* are about her.

To Petrarch, Laura represented physical and spiritual perfection, but, married with 11 children, she was unable to return his love. She died of the plague in 1348. Petrarch had two children by an unknown woman. His son, Giovanni, died in 1361 of the plague, while his daughter nursed him in his old age. He died in Arquà in 1374.

Petrarch was a great scholar. He searched out and discovered ancient classical manuscripts hidden in dusty libraries, and his correction, copying and interpretation of the classical authors gave tremendous impetus to the Renaissance. He was a friend of Simone Martini, who painted the frescoes at the Palais des Papes in Avignon (see p.38), and was popular amongst all the greats of the day.

47

and visit **Fontvieille**, famous for its well-preserved mill. (If you know Alphonse Daudet's *Lettres de mon Moulin*, this is where Maître Cornille tried to pretend that his mill was working at full speed, when its days were truly over.) There is no other scenery is so typically Provençal or beloved, but note that you won't be alone.

FONTAINE-DE-VAUCLUSE

Wedged between the Lubéron Mountains and Mont Ventoux, the town of Vaucluse (*Vallis clausa* – 'closed valley') gave its name to the *département*. **Fontaine-de-Vaucluse** is best seen in spring or winter, when the mysterious, little explained, underwater river suddenly swells and gushes out of its green grotto beneath the towering cliff. (The variation in the water level is spectacular: from 4,500 litres/990 gallons a second in the dry season, to 200,000 litres/44,000 gallons in autumn and spring.) In summer, a sound-and-light show explains the history and mystery of the phenomenon. This little town of 600 inhabitants attracts more than one million visitors a year.

Go up the **Chemin de la Fontaine** (a 10-minute walk) and see where Petrarch came to dream of Laura (see p.47). He himself said: 'How often did I rise at midnight ... at that hour alone, with a mingled sense of pleasure and horror did I enter that immense cavern from which the river gushes forth, a place men fear to enter even by daylight and with companions.'

Petrarch's monument in the main square was erected in 1804. His **museum**, built on the spot where he may have lived, has some documentation on the poet, his work, and Laura. Also here is the **Musée des Santons** (little Provençal figures), where you can admire the masterpiece of 39 figures carved in a single nutshell.

The poet Petrarch is said to haunt tiny Fontaine-de-Vaucluse on the banks of the River Sorgue.

L'ISLE-SUR-LA-SORGUE

Just beside Fontaine-de-Vaucluse, **L'Isle-sur-la-Sorgue** is criss-crossed by various arms of the River Sorgue, which parcel it into a neat and charming overgrown village (though much troubled by heavy traffic). Due to its canals, the town has been dubbed the 'Venice of the Comtat Venaissin'. An old, mossy water-wheel turns languorously in the public gardens of the *Caisse d'Épargne* bank, and old 16th- and 17th-century houses which overlook the canals give an idea of the wealth of the gentry in the town's heyday.

The **Hôtel-Dieu** (part hospital, part religious order), with its lovely entrance gate, was built between 1749 and 1757. The chapel has some fine 18th-century woodwork, as well as local Moustiers faience, and a monumental fountain playing majestically in the garden.

Arles and Southern Provence

ARLES

Although first impressions of **Arles** can be of a rather dishevelled and run-down place, this judgement is soon proven wrong. The sheer volume and consistency of the Roman remains and medieval treasures, combined with the charm of the Rhône-side setting, telescope centuries and civilizations into a definite 'must'.

Start off at the **Place de la République**, the heart of old Arles, with its Egyptian granite obelisk from the old Roman circus. On one side of the square stands the stately **Hôtel de Ville** (town hall, built 1673-84), and on the other the Église Saint-Trophime.

Two masterpieces of Provençal Romanesque art await the visitor. In the **Église Saint-Trophime**, where Good King René married his first queen, Jeanne de Laval, you can see Roman influences in the trium-

phal arch design of the splendid porch. Note the scenes, in particular the beautiful *Last Judgement* on the tympanum over the entrance, and the *12 Apostles* just below. Then go round to the elegant **cloister**, which was put up in two successive stages: during the 12th century (north), and during the 14th (south and west – where you enter). The differences are clear, the earlier Romanesque, the later Gothic. The cloister provides a haven of peace.

The **Museon Arlaten** next door is worth a visit for a wonderful picture of life in old Provence, when the sophisticated culture of the south contrasted with the simpler way of life in the north.

The few scattered ruins of the ancient **Théâtre** give only a pale idea of the once glorious structure which attracted visitors from throughout the Roman Empire. Built at the end of the 1st century BC, it served as a convenient quarry from the 5th century for the building of churches, ramparts and houses. In its prime, it had a vast elaborate stone 'wall' of

*T*he past and the present live happily side-by-side in Arles.

pillars and statues, with a sloping roof – yet another Roman acoustical technique – and it held 7,000 spectators.

It's easier to visualize proceedings in the **amphitheatre** (*arènes*), which seated over 20,000 in the days of the gladiators. For the most spectacular view, climb up to the broad path running along the roof of the arches. Started in 46 BC, the arena served as a kind of last defence when Arles was later besieged by Barbarians. Each floor has 60 arcades, and the ring itself measures 136m by 107m (446ft by 350ft).

Take the **Boulevard des Lices** – the avenue you have to see and be seen in – towards the south east of town. Here lie the melancholy remains of the **Alyscamps**, the Roman and medieval burial grounds Van Gogh liked to paint when he came to live in Arles in 1888. Only a few sarcophagi remain, in an avenue leading to the ruined Église Saint-Honorat. Several marvellous examples have found their way into the **Musée d'Art chrétien** in the former Jesuit chapel in town.

Saved at the eleventh hour, the Abbaye de Montmajour and its superb cloister.

You should not overlook the **Musée Réattu**, in the 15th-century Grand Priory of the Knights of Malta. It is brimming with Provençal art, and has drawings from the Picasso donation. Arles is also celebrated (by some) for its **Féria**, (bullfighting) and weekly contests are held in the amphitheatre in the summer.

ABBAYE DE MONTMAJOUR

Just 5km (3 miles) from Arles, on top of a hillock, stand the evocative ruins of the **Abbaye de Montmajour** (Van Gogh painted it many times). Below lie ricefields between the Alpilles and Crau mountains.

The 10th-century Benedictine monastery developed into an abbey. Religious troubles in the 14th century demanded the construction of the defence

52

tower (1369), still there today. In the Middle Ages, the idea of the *pardon de la Sainte-Croix* paid off, notably in 1409 as 150,000 pilgrims appeared, offering money for their 'pardon'. However the abbey fell on hard times, and Louis XVI had it dissolved in 1786. When sold off after the French Revolution, estate agents removed all the easily disposable parts. Those left were saved in the nick of time by lovers of Arles – restoration began in 1872.

L'Église de Notre-Dame itself is mostly 12th century Romanesque – it is the **cloister** that appeals to most visitors. Note the capitals, some Romanesque, some Gothic, most dating from around 1375. Try whispering in echoing **Sainte-Croix** chapel nearby.

TARASCON

Tarascon stood as an island in the Rhône and a Greek trading post until the Romans moved in, setting up camp where the present fortress now stands. The town is popular today for its revival of two old festivals, both of which stem from the legend of St Martha and the **53**

Tarasque (sea-dragon), during which St Martha tames the Tarasque by sprinkling it with holy water. Good King René inaugurated the Tarasque festival, which is now celebrated as the *Fêtes de la Tarasque* at Whitsun, and the *Fête de la Sainte Marthe* on 29 July.

The city has other claims to fame, including its forbidding **castle**, one of the great medieval fortresses still in France. King René used the existing Roman foundations to build it up in the 15th century, and it served as a prison until 1926. The corridors and king's apartments give a good impression of René's lifestyle at the height of his reign.

There is a superb **view** over Tarascon and the Rhône from the terrace, but it does mean climbing 136 steps. In 1794, Robespierre's prisoners appreciated the panorama somewhat less, as they hurtled headlong into the river below.

Tarascon initially resented the mythical 'hero' that writer Daudet gave it in *Tartarin de*

Shades of Van Gogh

Van Gogh wrote in a letter from Arles: 'Oh, the beautiful sun of midsummer! It beats upon my head, and I do not doubt that it makes one a little queer.' Arles inspired his most fertile period, but also triggered the frenzy in which he cut off an ear and had himself committed to an asylum in nearby Saint-Rémy. He died a year later back in the Paris suburb of Auvers. Today, the tourist office in the Boulevard des Lices provides a map tracing 30 of the sites he painted, or you can take the tour with a guide and commentary.

His house and favourite café have both gone, bombed in 1944, but the surrounding fields are still filled with the sunflowers and olive trees he loved to paint. The gardens of the Espace Van-Gogh in Arles have been laid out exactly as he would have seen them.

Tarascon: a vainglorious adventurer who made them, they felt, look like folkloric backwoodsmen. Nonetheless, Tartarin's reputation stuck to the town, and he is as linked to Tarascon today as Dick Whittington to London. Take a look at his **house**, a reconstruction of a late 19th-century bourgeois home, with plenty of background on Tartarin.

On the other side of the Rhône is **Beaucaire**, a lookalike château. Every July from 1217 until the arrival of train travel, it was the focus of Europe's biggest trade fair (some years it hosted 300,000 merchants). For a better idea of the event, drop into the **Musée du Vieux Beaucaire**, and climb up to the château's **tower** for a splendid view.

LA MONTAGNETTE

If you're on your way down from Avignon to Tarascon, try *not* to avoid **La Montagnette** (and equally the Abbaye de Saint-Michel-de-Frigolet), by taking the road through sleepy **Barbentane**. Worth visiting here is the handsome, 17th-century **château** – known to locals as 'the Petit Trianon in the Sun' – which offers excellent Louis XV and XVI furniture and superb Italian-style gardens, and is still owned by the Barbentane family.

As you climb towards the **Abbaye de Saint-Michel-de-Frigolet**, at the top of the Montagnette, you'll appreciate why the poor monks of Montmajour would come here from their marshy swamps for fresh air and a rest after a bout of malaria. They actually founded the abbey in the 10th century, and in the 11th century built the **chapel of Notre-Dame-de-Bon-Remède**, which still attracts an annual pilgrimage.

It was at Saint-Michel-de-Frigolet that Anne of Austria prayed to have a son. When her wish was finally granted in 1638, the world was blessed with Louis XIV, and in gratitude she donated the magnificent **wood panels**. Ownership of the complex kept changing following the Revolution, but it eventually fell into the hands of the Premontrian monks. **55**

THE CAMARGUE

A kind of small wedge or delta between the Petit Rhône and the Grand Rhône, where they part to meet the Mediterranean, the **Camargue** has been reclaimed from the sea to form a **national nature reserve** and modern resorts on the coast.

Despite its apparent drawbacks – such as flies and mosquitoes, totally flat surroundings (the highest point is only 4m/13ft), and unremitting heat – its appeal is strong, and for many it comes as a revelation. Here, wild ducks, pink flamingos and herons can be found, while horses and bulls dot the flats. The Camargue is captivating in its mystery, but it has to be discovered, either by foot or on horseback.

Villages are few and far between: starting at Arles, the road to Saintes-Maries-de-la-Mer hardly gives a cheerful picture of the region. With permission from the Directeur de la Réserve, la Capelière, Arles, you can stop and spend time in the nature reserve, which is popular with birdwatchers.

AIGUES-MORTES

History comes into its own in **Aigues-Mortes** (from *aquae mortuae*, 'dead waters' of the marshland). There are few grand monuments (although the ramparts in themselves are spectacular), but it is rare that you come across a town so evocative of its past.

When it was built, Aigues-Mortes lay on the sea. Under

The Camargue is a true paradise for horses. At its southern tip is the wayside cross at St-Maries-de-la-Mer.

pious Louis IX (St Louis), the 38 ships of the Seventh Crusade left from these city walls in 1248 for Cyprus, 23 sailing days away. For the best view of the site as it was, head first to Grau du Roi for about one mile (1.5km), and look back at the splendidly intact city.

The overall town plan has scarcely changed since Louis IX's planners laid it out in the mid-13th century. Today, silting has left the city 8km (5 miles) inland from the Mediterranean, its grid of streets and walls miraculously preserved.

Start your tour of the **ramparts** at Porte de la Gardette. The religious conflicts that affected this area are indelibly engraved here. The **Tour des Bourgignons** is named after the Bourgignons (Burgundy), who one night in 1418, during the Hundred Years' War, were massacred in their sleep by the Armagnacs, who piled up their corpses in the tower, salted them and left them to moulder.

From the top of the tower, there is a lovely **view** to the sea beyond. Beside the good craft shops situated on **Place Saint-Louis** is the **church** reputed to be the one in which Louis IX prayed before he set out for the Holy Land.

SAINTES-MARIES-DE-LA-MER

Situated at the southern tip of the Camargue, the town of **Saintes-Maries-de-la-Mer** is something of a mirage after the flat landscape. Legend has **57** it that the Virgin Mary and Mary Magdalene, along with their servant Sara, landed on this spot before they set off to evangelize Provence. One of the Marys stayed on with Sara, and was buried in the church of Saintes-Maries-de-la-Mer.

The ensuing cult's first pilgrims were gypsies and no-mads – gypsy tradition contin-ues today. In the crypt of the extraordinary **fortress-church** are a reliquary and a strange, costumed statue of Sara. Each May, after a night vigil in the crypt, the statues of the saints in their little boats are carried aloft by gypsies to the sea in a spirit of intense religious fervour. Go up to the church roof for a superb **view** of the sea and the town, including the seaside *arènes* (bullring).

Scaling the Heights of Faith

Throughout this area of the Midi, Protestants were known as *camisards* (owing to the white over-shirt worn as a recogniz-able sign). Following the Revocation of the Edict of Nantes (1685), in which Louis XIV stripped Protestants of all religious and civil liberties, the inhabitants were forced to live for the most part in the remote Cévennes Mountains, where they prac-tised their faith in hiding.

Some of their exploits in the grim *Tour de Constance* in Aigues-Mortes, where many of them were imprisoned, became famous. One such was that of Abraham Mazel, who with 16 others made an epic escape attempt in 1705 after spending 10 months chiselling a way out, while his companions sang psalms to cover the noise. Marie Durand was imprisoned for 38 years in the tower, obstinately refusing to foreswear her faith (you can still see the word *résister* (resist), which she engraved on a stone beside an air hole). Her fortitude was an inspiration to all Protestants, and the governor of Languedoc finally released her in 1768, when he learned of her plight and realized her indomitable courage.

The Lubéron

 CAVAILLON

Cavaillon, home of France's most succulent cantaloupe melons, lies in a protected site, sheltered by rugged rocks – the Colline Saint-Jacques. The town provides a perfect starting point for various destinations: the Alpilles mountains, the Lubéron area, Gordes (see p.63), and Fontaine-de-Vaucluse (see p.48).

Like any respectable Provençal town, Cavaillon has its lst-century **triumphal arch** – or at least half of it – a sober monument, but profusely decorated. The former **cathedral Saint-Véran** is in typically Provençal style, with an apse containing lovely woodwork, as well as a charming 12th-century cloister.

For the Jewish community, the Comtat Venaissin was one of the rare parts of France where they could live free of persecution, and the fairly opulent **synagogue** gives an idea of the community's success.

UP AND DOWN THE LUBÉRON

Striking out from Cavaillon, head east to the **Montagne de Lubéron**, the heart of the Provençal countryside and a protected regional park. From Cavaillon to Manosque, the mountain chain stretches like a necklace for 65km (40 miles) and culminates at a height of 1,125m (3,690ft). The valleys are carpeted with lavender, while the *garrigue* scrubland shimmers with every colour of the Mediterranean.

Perched on a spur of rock, the village **Oppède-le-Vieux** has been rescued from its ruins by writers and artists seeking a residence off the beaten track. The ruins themselves have become crazy shapes that blend into the tortured landscape.

The village gate gives an idea of the glory of this citadel before its deliberate destruction in the Wars of Religion against the Vaudois (see p.19). In particular, the ruins of the castle (which was built in 1209 by the count of Toulouse) have a grand, if austere appearance. **59**

Ménerbes sits on top of its hill like a ship sailing above the valley, dominated by a medieval fortress which served as the Protestants' last redoubt in the 16th century. It resisted a siege for over a year. Behind the church at the far end of town, there is a fine view over the mountains to the Vaucluse plateau and the distant peak of Mont Ventoux. Have a look in the **church**, with its pleasing 17th-century altar.

The tower and ruins of the sinister fortress perched on the brow of the hill at charming **Lacoste**, formerly belonged to the family of the equally sinister Marquis de Sade, up until 1777. He spent seven fairly tempestuous years here (1771-78), before his somewhat un-Christian conduct led him to the Bastille. After his death his concierge bought the château.

Bonnieux, 6km (3.5 miles) beyond, juts out over the Coulon valley. Not being a Protestant village, it never suffered persecution. Curling up the hill, it has kept some of its 13th- and 14th-century walls, and the town hall occupies a

The vibrant ochre of the quarries of the Chaussée des Géants (Giants' Causeway) at Roussillon.

lovely old *hôtel*. The view from the terrace on the hill behind the town hall is stunning: in the distance is Mont Ventoux, while to the north west are Gordes (see p.63) and the rust-coloured ravines around Roussillon (see p.63).

The **Musée de la Boulangerie** offers an interesting insight into the history of bread production – a serious business in France.

Forge on to the **Fort de Buoux**, where the trail peters out. You can see the fantastic strategic position of the overgrown fort and ruined village, and note the prehistoric shelter and tombs dug out of the rock. The complex was dismantled by Louis XIV, as a punishment for harbouring Protestants.

Down now to **Lourmarin**, a delightful, gentle, valley town, at the point where the Grand and Petit Lubéron meet and

split. In the romantic cemetery lies the grave of writer Albert Camus, who loved the town. Lourmarin's **château**, lying a short distance outside, belongs to the Académie of Aix-en-Provence, and has been turned into a kind of 'Villa Medici' for creative minds. The main wing dates from the mid-16th century and includes a remarkable staircase. The apartments have been beautifully furnished with Provençal furniture.

Hop across the Durance to the **Abbaye de Silvacane**. Although not deep in a wood or hidden like the other two of Provence's 'three sisters' (see Sénanque, p.64), it was nonetheless hard to reach along the formerly marshy banks (*Silvacane* means 'wood of reeds'). The original church dates from 1175-1230, while the cloister dates from the late 13th century. The buildings slope down gently towards the river. **61**

Gordes – just as pretty from afar as close to, with the Vasarely Foundation in the château.

Cadenet has charm, and **Ansouis** a formidable château, which belonged to Elzéar and Dauphine de Sabran (a distinguished family of the Midi) in the 13th-14th century – both later became saints. Visit the **Chambre des Saints**, the **dining room** hung with Flemish tapestries, and the **kitchen**, with its old utensils.

Also here are some beautiful hanging gardens with box, cypress and maritime pines, among others, in carefully designed arrangements.

There's plenty of dramatic scenery on the way to Manosque in Haute-Provence. **Cucuron**, on which the writer Daudet based his mythical village of *Cu-cu-gnan*, and where the church pulpit is made of multicoloured marble; then **La Tour-d'Aigues**, with the imposing ruins of a Renaissance castle; **Pertuis** where the well-loved Queen Jeanne 'owns' one of the many old houses in the centre; and finally **Mirabeau**, where a bridge spanning the River Durance links four *départements*.

LUBÉRON KALEIDOSCOPE

On the main road from Cavaillon to Apt (N100), about 8km (5 miles) along, take a small turning to **Pont Julien** (named in honour of Julius Caesar) over the River Coulon (called *Cavalon* in local parlance). This Roman bridge, with its three graceful arches, has lasted nearly two millennia. The holes in the upper part are there to let the water through if it should rise suddenly.

To set off the startling red of the rust-coloured ravines, the villagers of **Roussillon** paint their houses every imaginable shade of ochre (17 at the last count), from gold to vermilion, through brown and pink. This makes for a vivid, outrageously picturesque village. You may like to walk round the Colorado de Rustrel, some 10km (6.5 miles) to the north, to see the quarries from where the ochre originates.

Its dramatic location, looking across to the Lubéron from the southern edge of the Vaucluse plateau, has made the village of **Gordes** one of the most prosperous in the region, with its popular boutiques and galleries, and the **Vasarely Foundation**, a diverse collection of the Hungarian-French painter's Op and Pop works, displayed in several cavernous rooms of a former château.

The houses hug the hillside on steep, winding streets, leading up to a 12th-century **castle** and massive **church** at the top. Gourmet restaurants as well as quality shops and art galleries are the trappings of a highly **63** successful tourist town, plus a varied collection of museums. Of the 1,600 inhabitants of the village, in part destroyed and abandoned during the last war, only 200 are 'real' locals, the rest having been drawn by the stunning setting. From here, look across at the hazy, blue panorama of the Lubéron.

South west of Gordes (2km/ 1 mile) is the strange **Village des Bories**, with its old dry-stone cabins (*bories*) grouped round a baker's oven, serving as a museum of rural life. There are 500 *bories* scattered around Provence, their origins now lost in history, but these are the most complete.

A short drive north west of Gordes on the D177 takes you down to the exquisite, 12th-century Cistercian **Abbaye de Sénanque**, nestling in a valley of lavender fields. The monks abandoned the abbey after the 17th century, but it has been in use again since 1989. The Cistercians are noted for their sober architecture and ascetic way of life. Sénanque, founded in 1147, is perhaps the most **64** admirable of Provence's 'three (Cistercian) sisters', which include Sylvacane (see p.61) and Le Thoronet.

The Romanesque **cloister** here has been beautifully restored for summer art-shows, while the refectory provides an audio-visual guide to monastic, and specifically Cistercian, life. The permanent exhibition is, somewhat surprisingly, on the Tuaregs (nomads) of the Sahara, while the 17th-century **kitchens** are now a museum of Romanesque architecture. Try to be at the abbey at mass for the compellingly mystical atmosphere.

Apt is a quite unpretentious town and a good centre for Lubéron excursions. Its main claim to fame these days is as the home of much-prized candied fruits (*fruits confits*). Visit the Saturday **market** for a feel of 'real' Provence, where sun-seekers, intellectuals and farmers mix happily amidst the stalls. You should also find time to visit the **Église Sainte-Anne**, which through a variety of architectural styles chronicles the historic development of Apt in a nutshell.

A Selection of Hotels and Restaurants in Provence

Recommended Hotels and Restaurants

The range of hotels in Provence runs the gamut of very luxurious to very reasonable, even if the region is not among the cheapest in the country.

The following list is selective, and our criteria are price range and a geographical spread of locations. In hotels, the following symbols apply for a double room with bath but without breakfast:

IIII	above 1,500F
II	500-1,500F
I	below 500F

(There are, however, considerable variations, with perfectly acceptable rooms at 250F as well as luxury rooms over 3,000F.)

For restaurants, the following symbols apply for a full meal for two with a reasonable bottle of wine:

IIII	above 400F
II	200-400F
I	below 200F

(This doesn't rule out the multitude of restaurants with an excellent fixed menu at lunchtime.)

Advance booking is always recommended in small establishments, but even in bigger ones in town, both in and out of season (particularly during the big festivals), it's worth it.

AIGUES-MORTES

Arcades ⫼

23, boulevard Gambetta,
30220 Aigues-Mortes
Tel. 66 53 81 13
Fax 66 53 75 46
Restaurant in a lovely old 16th-century house, serving local specialities outside in the garden.

AIX-EN-PROVENCE

Caravelle ⫶

29, boulevard du Roi-René,
13090 Aix-en-Provence
Tel. 42 21 53 05
Fax 42 96 55 46
Often full because of its value for money. Rooms on the garden side are a bit quieter. No restaurant.

Château de la Pioline   ▌▌▌
13290 on A51 at Milles
Tel. 42 20 07 81
Fax 42 59 96 12
A château classified as a historical monument, with a garden *à la française*, a swimming pool and a restaurant in a magnificent setting.

Grand Hôtel   ▌▌
Nègre Coste
33, cours Mirabeau,
13090 Aix-en-Provence
Tel. 42 27 74 22
Fax 42 26 80 93
Well-run hotel with high standards, excellently located in the centre of town. No restaurant.

Hôtel des Augustins   ▌▌
3, rue de la Masse,
13090 Aix-en-Provence
Tel. 42 27 28 59
Fax 42 26 74 87
Formerly Convent of the Grands-Augustins, situated in old Aix, beside the Cours Mirabeau. Luxuriously redecorated and furnished with Louis XIII-style furniture. No restaurant.

Hôtel le Manoir   ▌▌
8, rue d'Entrecasteaux,
13090 Aix-en-Provence
Tel. 42 26 27 20
Fax 42 27 17 97
This hotel was formerly a monastery, and is very comfortably furnished. A magnificent section of cloister has been kept – breakfast is served there.

Mas d'Entremont   ▌▌
13090 3km (2 miles) out on
the N7 at Celony
Tel. 42 23 45 32
Fax 42 21 15 83
Luxurious, Provençal-style country house, in a park overlooking Aix, with terraces and swimming pool. High quality cuisine in an idyllic setting.

Le Pigonnet   ▌▌
5, rue Pigonnet,
13090 Aix-en-Provence
Tel. 42 59 02 90
Fax 42 59 47 77
Charming old house set in a park with a swimming pool, slightly outside the centre of town, but very peaceful. The hotel restaurant, *Le Patio*, provides some first-class cuisine.

Résidence Rotonde   ▌
15, avenue des Belges,
13090 Aix-en-Provence
Tel. 42 26 29 88
Fax 42 38 66 98
Charming historic house with a 14th-century cloister. Slightly outside the town centre, but good value nonetheless. No restaurant.   **67**

APT

Auberge du Lubéron

17, quai Léon Sagy, 84400 Apt
Tel. 90 74 12 50
Fax 90 04 79 49
Pleasant little hotel with 15 rooms and all the requisite comforts. Attractive restaurant serving Provençal specialities out in the garden.

Relais de Roquefure

84400 6km (4 miles) from Apt by N100
Tel. 90 04 88 88
Unpretentious and well kept hotel in a calm spot in a park. Meals served outdoors.

ARLES

Hostellerie des Arènes

62, rue du Refuge,
13200 Arles
Tel. 90 96 13 05
Right beside the *arènes* (bullring), this modest, family-style restaurant serves first-class meals, with attentive service and care, down to the simplest dishes. A chance for a really good *daube provençale*.

Hôtel d'Arlatan

26, rue du Sauvage,
13200 Arles
Tel. 90 93 56 66
Fax 90 49 68 45
Former private *hôtel* of the Comte d'Arlatan de Beaumont. Beautiful furniture and much charm, with great character and refined comfort to accompany it.

Hôtel Calendal

22, place Pomme,
13200 Arles
Tel. 90 96 11 89
Comfortable family hotel, whose rooms look out over either the amphitheatre or a pleasant garden in which breakfast is served.

Hôtel le Cloître

18, rue du Cloître,
13200 Arles
Tel. 90 96 29 50
Fax 90 96 02 88
Hotel with all the charm of the provinces, tucked away beside a tiny uphill road. Comfortable, renovated rooms.

Hôtel Mireille

2, place Saint-Pierre,
13200 Arles
Tel. 90 93 70 74
Fax 90 93 87 28
Very spacious and comfortable rooms in this hotel situated on the other side of the Rhône. There's a delightful view out over a private swimming pool, which is sheltered by a row of trees from the road. In addition, there's also a

huge dining room, with a high standard of cuisine. Free parking and a garage.

Jules César   ▮▮▮

boulevard des Lices,
13200 Arles
Tel. 90 93 43 20
Fax 90 93 33 47

A former 17th-century Carmelite Convent, with interior garden. Superb comfort and great charm, with swimming pool.

Mas de la Chapelle   ▮▮

petite route de Tarascon,
13200 Arles
Tel. 90 93 23 15
Fax 90 96 53 74

In an exceptional setting 5km (3 miles) from Arles is this wonderful 16th-century house in a very beautiful park. There are swimming pools and tennis courts, and the restaurant is in the former chapel of the Knights of Malta. Emanating from within is refined cuisine with a pronounced Provençal flavour.

Le Vaccarès   ▮▮

place du Forum (1ᵉʳ étage)
Tel. 90 96 06 71

Light, balanced and innovative cuisine, with specialities such as *loup à la vapeur avec compote d'orange et citron à l'huile d'olive* (something of a mouthful in all senses) or *vinaigrette de rougets aux aubergines*.

AVIGNON

Auberge de Cassagne   ▮▮

(at the Avignon-Nord exit from the A4 Motorway)
450 allée de Cassagne,
at Pontet 84130
Tel. 90 31 04 13
Fax 90 32 25 09

This establishment has the discreet charm of an old Provençal house, in a magnificent garden with a swimming pool. Internationally famous cuisine, with a delicate touch of Provence.

Brunel   ▮▮▮

46, rue de Balance,
84000 Avignon
Tel. 90 85 24 83
Fax 90 86 26 67

Excellent cuisine with, in particular, *morue* (cod) *fraîche aux épices, rouget piperade en tapenade*, and *ratatouille d'agneau*.

Cité des Papes   ▮

1, rue Jean-Vilar,
84000 Avignon
Tel. 90 86 44 25
Fax 90 27 39 21

Handsome, air-conditioned rooms in a new, centrally located (near **69** the Palais des Papes) hotel. Small café below serving its speciality – ice-creams. No restaurant.

Europe ▯▯▯

12, place Crillon,
84000 Avignon
Tel. 90 82 66 92
Fax 90 85 43 66

16th-century house near the Palais des Papes whose restaurant, the *Vieille Fontaine*, offers beautifully prepared Provençal specialities.

Hostellerie les Agassins ▯▯

Route de Lyon, at Pontet 84130
Tel. 90 32 42 91
Fax 90 32 08 29

Five minutes from Avignon, in a flower park with a swimming pool, this modern hotel has 25 tastefully decorated rooms. Restaurant with all the flavour of Provence on your plate.

Hostellerie les Frênes ▯▯▯

645, avenue les Vertes Rives,
84140 Montfavet
Tel. 90 31 17 93
Fax 90 23 95 03

At the gates of Avignon, in a shady park with trees of a venerable age, plus a swimming pool and a 19th-century manor house with old furniture, as well as excellent and original cuisine.

Hôtel d'Angleterre ▯

29, boulevard Raspail,
84000 Avignon
Tel. 90 86 34 31
Fax 90 86 86 74

Splendid former *hôtel* with 40 very reasonably priced and sizeable rooms in a quiet area of town. Parking inside the courtyard.

Hôtel Bristol ▯

44, avenue Jean-Jaurès,
84000 Avignon
Tel. 90 82 21 21
Fax 90 86 22 72

Family-run hotel with air-conditioned rooms with television and minibar. Garage, sauna. Near the station. Closed in February.

La Mirande ▯▯▯

4, place Amirande,
84000 Avignon
Tel. 90 85 93 93
Fax 90 96 26 85

Private 17th-century *hôtel*, right in the centre of town, at the foot of the walls, luxuriously furnished.

Le Petit Bedon ▯

70, rue Joseph-Vernet,
84000 Avignon
Tel. 90 82 33 98

Excellent Provençal cuisine with copious helpings in a pleasant, if fairly routine setting. Try one of the specialities: calf sweetbread *à la moutarde* with kidney 'petals'. Prices are very reasonable for the quality.

LES BAUX-DE-PROVENCE

La Benvengudo ▌▌

South west of Les Baux
on the D78
Tel. 90 54 32 54
Fax 90 54 42 58
Luxury hotel with 17 rooms in the buildings of a solid Provençal *bastide*, in a large and magnificent garden with a swimming pool. First-class regional cuisine.

La Cabro d'Or ▌▌

13520 Les Baux-de-Provence
Tel. 90 54 33 21
Fax 90 54 45 98
A typical and charming Provençal *mas* (farmhouse) with 22 rooms, a big flowered garden and swimming pool. Provençal specialities, excellently prepared.

Hostellerie de la Reine Jeanne ▌

At entry to the old village,
13520 Les-Baux-de-Provence
Tel. 90 54 32 06
Nice little hotel with 11 rooms and a lovely view, especially from the dining room, down over the Val d'Enfer. Good cuisine.

L'Oustau de Baumanière ▌▌▌

13250 Les Baux-de-Provence
Tel. 90 54 33 07
Fax 90 54 40 46
Old, 16th-century house, redecorated in excellent taste. Flowered terraces and a garden (riding and swimming possibilities). Some of the best cuisine in France, as well as marvellous wines.

Mas d'Aigret ▌▌

East of Les Baux-de-Provence
on the D27
Tel. 90 54 33 54
Fax 90 54 41 37
Restaurant lying at the foot of the ruins, in a very calm spot. Garden with a swimming pool. Fine regional cuisine served in the troglodyte restaurant. 14 rooms.

BONNIEUX

L'Aigle Brun ▌▌

6km (4 miles) from Bonnieux by
D36, 84480 Bonnieux
Tel. 90 74 04 14
A little estate lost amid the spreading trees in a vale of the Lubéron. Regional cuisine with specialities.

Hostellerie du Prieuré ▌

84480 Bonnieux
Tel. 90 75 80 78
Former 17th-century priory in a **71**

pleasant setting at the foot of the ramparts. 10 rooms with refined decor. Good cuisine, with meals served outside in the garden during the summer.

CARPENTRAS

Blason de Provence

At Montheux, 4km (2.5 miles)
south west by D942,
84170 Montheux
Tel. 90 66 31 34
Fax 90 66 83 05
Pretty Provençal house in a lovely setting with swimming pool and tennis courts. 20 very comfortable rooms and excellent cuisine.

Hôtel le Fiacre

153, rue Vigne,
84200 Carpentras
Tel. 90 63 03 15
An old private *hôtel* with a monumental staircase and a pleasant central patio. 20 very comfortable rooms.

Sélect

At Montheux, 4km (2.5 miles)
south west by D942,
84170 Carpentras
Tel. 90 66 27 91
Pleasant and comfortable small establishment set in a garden with a swimming pool. 8 rooms. Light, good cuisine.

CAVAILLON

Fin du Siècle

46, plan du Clos (1er etage),
84300 Cavaillon
Tel. 90 71 12 27
A comfortable first-floor restaurant serving refined, regional and light cuisine, giving particularly good value for money.

Hôtel Christel

2km (1 mile) from Cavaillon on
the road to Tarascon,
84300 Cavaillon
Tel. 90 71 07 79
Fax 90 78 27 94
Biggish hotel with 104 rooms, forming a pleasant complex with swimming pool and tennis courts. Good quality cuisine.

Hôtel du Parc

place du Clos, 84300 Cavaillon
Tel. 90 71 57 78
Fax 90 76 10 35
Right in the centre of Cavaillon, with 40 bright and comfortable rooms. No restaurant.

CHÂTEAUNEUF-DU-PAPE

Hostellerie Château des Fines Roches

3km (2 miles) south of town by
D17, 84230 Châteauneuf-du-Pape

Tel. 90 83 70 23
Fax 90 83 78 42
The château lies within a vineyard, and has a quite superb view. The rooms (only seven) are all sumptuously decorated. Excellent regional cuisine that justifies its good reputation.

CUCURON

L'Etang
84160 Cucuron
Tel. 90 77 21 25
In the village which inspired the writer Alphonse Daudet, this hotel lies beside a pool which is framed by trees, providing a calm and restful setting. Its 8 rooms are all very comfortable, and the restaurant's cuisine has that jolly Provençal touch to it; try the Lubéron lamb (*agneau*).

FONTAINE-DE-VAUCLUSE

Hostellerie du Château
Quartier Petit Place,
84800 Fontaine-de-Vaucluse
Tel. 90 20 31 54
The veranda of this slightly old-fashioned and small family hotel stands over the famous river and its paddlewheels. The exquisite house speciality is *lotte moutarde à l'ancienne*.

Hôtel du Parc
84800 Fontaine-de-Vaucluse
Tel. 90 20 31 57
The terrace above the River Sorgue is delightful, and this little family-run hotel with 12 comfortable rooms is seductive.

FONTVIEILLE

Le Patio
117, route du Nord,
13990 Fontvieille
Tel. 90 54 73 10
In a former sheep pen, serving delicious Provençal specialities, and grilled meats over a wood fire.

La Regalido
rue Frédéric Mistral,
13990 Fontvieille
Tel. 90 54 60 22
Fax 90 54 64 29
A former mill, nicely restored in a flower garden, with 14 charming rooms. Plenty of inspiration in the cuisine, such as *nage de loup à l'huile d'olive et gros sel*.

GIGONDAS

Les Florets
1.5km (1 mile) from the village
by Route des Dentelles
Tel. 90 65 85 91
Fax 90 65 83 80
Set deep in the countryside, this **73**

pretty hotel has 13 comfortable rooms and plenty of peace and tranquillity. The view is out over the Dentelles de Montmirail. The regional cuisine is good and is served in the garden in summer.

GORDES

La Bastide de Gordes ▮▮▮
In the village,
84220 Gordes
Tel. 90 72 12 12
Fax 90 72 05 20
Beautifully renovated Provençal house with 18 rooms, each with tasteful décor. Superb view out over the Lubéron. Inspired cuisine with local Provençal specialities.

Domaine de l'Enclos ▮▮▮
route de Sénanque,
84220 Gordes
Tel. 90 72 08 22
Fax 90 72 03 03
A group of adorable little houses in the heart of the Lubéron. Park with swimming pool and tennis courts – a haven of peace. 14 well decorated rooms and four apartments. Cuisine with very refined local specialities.

Domaine le Moulin Blanc ▮▮
Chemin du Moulin-les-Baumettes,
84220 Gordes

Tel. 90 72 34 50
Fax 90 72 25 41
Former coaching inn and flour mill, with 18 rooms with delightful decor and furnishings. Park with swimming pool and tennis courts. First-rate cuisine.

Hôtel le Gordos ▮
1.5km (1 mile) out of Gordes on the road to Cavaillon
Tel. 90 72 00 75
Recently built and very comfortable *mas* (farmhouse). Pretty garden with swimming pool and patio for breakfast.

Mas de Tourteron ▮▮▮
Les Imberts,
84220 Gordes
Tel. 90 72 00 16
Lovely garden overlooking the immense Lubéron, with an excellent cuisine that goes by seasonal produce.

La Mayanelle ▮
20, route de la Combe,
84220 Gordes
Tel. 90 72 00 28
Perched on the flank of a mountain, the hotel offers a stunning view of the Lubéron, with 10 very comfortable rooms. The dining room is delightfully decorated and the cuisine includes several Provençal specialities.

L'ISLE-SUR-LA-SORGUE

Araxe Hôtel

*1.5km (1 mile) north on RN100
(the road towards Apt),
84800 l'Isle-sur-la-Sorgue
Tel. 90 38 40 00
Fax 90 20 84 74*

On the edge of town, this hotel's 47 comfortable rooms and 3 apartments represent one of the bigger establishments within a convenient perimeter. No restaurant.

Hostellerie la Grangette

*84800 l'Isle-sur-la-Sorgue
Tel. 90 20 00 77
Fax 90 20 07 06*

With a lovely shady park, a swimming pool and tennis courts, this excellent hotel has 15 rooms and an excellent view.

LOURMARIN

Hostellerie le Paradou

*84160 Lourmarin
Tel. 90 68 04 05*

Small hotel (9 rooms only), but excellent value for money, located at the entrance of the gorges, in among the trees. You can eat the hearty meals in the dining room, on the veranda, or on the terrace, which gives onto a field (ideal for children to play in).

Le Moulin de Lourmarin

*84160 Lourmarin
Tel. 90 68 06 69
Fax 90 68 31 76*

A small but very select and attractive establishment in this lovely little town, with only 17 rooms and three apartments.

MALAUCÈNE

L'Origan

*84340 Malaucène
Tel. 90 65 27 08*

In the centre of this typical Provençal village, and with the market just below its windows, this pleasant little hotel with views of Mont Ventoux is convenient for excursions in the region.

MANOSQUE

Hostellerie de la Fuste

*At le Fuste, 6.5km (4 miles) south east of Manosque on the D4,
04210 Valensole
Tel. 92 72 05 95
Fax 92 72 92 93*

Situated in a delightful park, with 14 rooms, swimming and tennis available. There's also a small but quite magnificent restaurant which offers game specialities in season among other excellent regional Provençal dishes.

75

Le François I ▮

18, rue Guilhem Pierre,
04100 Manosque
Tel. 92 72 07 99
A modern and comfortable hotel with 75 rooms at affordable rates. No restaurant.

Le Provence ▮

Route de Durance,
04100 Manosque
Tel. 92 72 39 38
Decorated in a modern style, with its own private car-park and swimming pool. The restaurant serves good, reasonably priced menus.

MARSEILLE

Calypso ▮▮

3, rue des Catalans,
13007 Marseille
Tel. 91 52 64 22
High quality, fresh and well prepared seafood dishes served in hearty proportions in very pleasant surroundings.

Concorde Parade ▮▮▮▮

11, rue de Mazargues,
13008 Marseille
Tel. 91 76 51 11
Fax 91 77 95 10
A few minutes away from the Vieux Port, 100 very comfortable rooms, with a shopping gallery built into the hotel.

Hôtel Lutetia ▮

38, allée Gambetta,
13001 Marseille
Tel. 91 50 81 78
In a calm street, a charming little hotel with a bright entry hall and 29 comfortable rooms.

Michel ▮▮▮

6, rue des Catalans,
13007 Marseille
Tel. 91 52 64 22
Great for fish of the day, and those two Marseille specialities, *bourride* and *bouillabaisse*.

Le Petit Nice ▮▮▮

Anse de Maldonné,
corniche JF Kennedy,
13007 Marseille
Tel. 91 59 25 92
Fax 91 59 28 08
Between two *calanques*, and in a beautiful site, the villas overlook the seawater swimming pool. 15 dream rooms and a well-furnished interior. Superb cuisine.

Le Vieux Port (Sofitel) ▮▮▮

36, boulevard Chemin Livon,
13007 Marseille
Tel. 91 52 90 19
Fax 91 31 46 52
127 superbly comfortable rooms, with swimming pool. Panoramic restaurant with view over the old port. Fine and imaginative cuisine.

MÉNERBES

Hostellerie le   IIII
Roy Soleil
Route de Beaumettes,
84560 Ménerbes
Tel. 90 72 25 61
Fax 90 72 36 55
In a truly perfect site, a delightful, 17th-century house lost within the vineyards. 14 pleasant rooms and a terrace in the garden. Exceptional cuisine including several Provençal specialities.

MONTMIRAIL

Montmirail   II
On road to Vacqueyras,
84190 Montmirail
Tel. 90 65 84 01
Fax 90 65 81 50
In a haven of peace beneath the fascinating peaks, with a pool in the garden, 46 rooms of great charm and comfort. The cuisine is typically Provençal.

ORANGE

Au Bec Fin   I
14, rue Ségmond-Weber,
84100 Orange
Tel. 90 34 14 76
The tables spill out over the narrow little street, while the parking is beside the pedestrian-only zone, at this pleasant little restaurant in front of the Theatre. Provençal specialities, like *poutargue provençale* (spiced fish roe).

Hôtel Arène   I
place de Langes,
84100 Orange
Tel. 90 34 10 95
Fax 90 34 91 62
Right in the centre of town, very near the pleasant place de la Mairie, but nonetheless quiet, this hotel has 30 sizeable rooms, and provides very good value for what is quite luxurious comfort. No restaurant.

Le Pigraillet   I
Colline Sainte-Eutrope,
84100 Orange
Tel. 90 34 44 25
Definitely the place for a superb meal, in a wooded park, overlooking the Rhône Valley, and all for a modest price. Warm welcome and cool swimming pool, plus flat-fee meal. Quite chic. Closed on Sunday.

Mas des Aigras   II
2km (1 mile) along N7 and turn off to Aigras,
84100 Orange
Tel. 90 34 81 01
A small establishment (11 rooms only), but in a really characteristic **77**

Provençal *mas* (farmhouse), this will enchant those that are looking for peace in a typical setting. Tennis and swimming available.

PERNES-LES-FONTAINES

L'Hermitage
2km (1 mile) by D938,
84210 Pernes-les-Fontaines
Tel. 90 66 51 41
Fax 90 61 36 41
Extremely restful hotel with 20 rooms set in a park some 6km (4 miles) from Carpentras.

ROUSSILLON

Mas de Garrigon
3km (2 miles) by C7,
84220 Roussillon
Tel. 90 05 63 22
Fax 90 05 70 01
Small hotel (7 rooms) and restaurant, but everything of top class standard, refined and tasteful, with a superb view over the Lubéron area from the delightful village of Roussillon. Advance booking is highly recommended.

Résidence les Ocres
Route de Gordes,
84220 Roussillon
Tel. 90 05 60 50
Small and without a restaurant,

but good value for money. Several of the 15 rooms enjoy a superb view. Excellent welcome.

SAINTES-MARIES-DE-LA-MER

Hippocampe
rue Camille Pelletan,
13460 Saintes-Maries-de-la-Mer
Tel. 90 97 80 91
A chance to taste local cuisine in a pleasant setting; the regional, 'classical' *menu* offers a delicious *bourride de lotte*, but there's plenty of choice.

Mas du Tardonne
3km (2 miles) north on the Arles road D570,
13460 Saintes-Maries-de-la-Mer
Tel. 90 97 93 11
Fax 90 97 71 04
Outside jacuzzi, sports gymnasium, and swimming pool. 19 delightful rooms. The cuisine has all the flavour of Provence.

SAINT-RÉMY-DE-PROVENCE

Les Antiques
15, avenue Pasteur,
13210 Saint-Rémy-de-Provence
Tel. 90 92 03 02

Fax 90 92 50 40
Beautiful house with very elegant, country-style decoration. Nearby park with swimming pool.

Canto Cigalo

chemin du Canto Cigalo,
13210 Saint-Rémy-de-Provence
Tel. 90 92 14 28
Fax 90 92 18 56
A view over the Alpilles Mountains is only one advantage of this modern, well-run hotel, which is particularly quiet and restful. The 20 rooms are pleasant and airy. No restaurant.

Château de Roussan

2km (1 mile) on the
Tarascon road,
13210 Saint-Rémy-de-Provence
Tel. 90 92 11 63
Fax 90 92 37 32
This splendid, 18th-century dwelling set in a park has been turned into a superbly furnished hotel, with 12 rooms.

Hostellerie du Vallon de Valrugues

chemin Canto Cigalo by D99,
13210 Saint-Rémy-de-Provence
Tel. 90 92 04 40
Fax 90 92 04 41
A magnificent hotel offering 41 rooms and 12 apartments, and a flowered terrace beside a swimming pool. The food is equally grand; try the saddle of lamb *aux senteurs des garrigues* for a bit of the local flavour.

SALON-DE-PROVENCE

Abbaye de Sainte-Croix

5km (3 miles) north east of
Salon by D17,
13330 Salon-de-Provence
Tel. 90 56 24 55
Fax 90 56 31 12
Offering 19 luxurious rooms in a former abbey, with conference facilities and all conceivable refinements. A renowned restaurant with specialities such as *gigotin de lotte panné aux truffes* and *roulade de lapereau aux anchois*.

Craponne

146, allée Craponne,
13330 Salon-de-Provence
Tel. 90 53 23 92
Meals are served outside in summer at this lovely restaurant with excellent cuisine and a special *menu* for children.

SÉGURET

La Table du Comtat

84110 Séguret
Tel. 90 46 91 49
Fax 90 46 94 27

Treat yourself to wonderful views out over the plain from the delightful hilltop village of Séguret. World-renowned cuisine with specialities (in summer) such as *filets de rouget barbet poêlés*, and the local *côte d'agneau* and *filet mignon*. 8 very smart rooms.

TARASCON

Le Provence ▮▮
7, boulevard Victor Hugo,
13150 Tarascon
Tel. 90 91 06 43
Fax 90 43 58 13
11 vast and air-conditioned rooms with proportionately huge bathrooms, each with its own terrace. Remarkably reasonable prices for the luxury and refinement offered. No restaurant.

VAISON-LA-ROMAINE

Hôtellerie du Beffroi ▮
rue de l'Echevé (Haute-Ville),
84110 Vaison-la-Romaine
Tel. 90 36 04 71
Fax 90 36 24 78
A fine, authentic 16th-century manorhouse. The rooms have all the size and comfort of old times, and are beautifully furnished. The hotel is situated in the less noisy, upper, medieval part of Vaison-la-Romaine.

VILLENEUVE-LÈS-AVIGNON

Atelier ▮
5, rue de la Foire,
30400 Villeneuve-lès-Avignon
Tel. 90 25 01 84
Fax 90 25 80 06
Within a 16th-century house, the 19 rooms are decorated with the charm of times gone by. There is a terrace on the roof for dining in clement (it usually is) weather, and a patio for delightful breakfasts outside.

Hostellerie du Vieux Moulin ▮
rue du Vieux Moulin,
30400 Villeneuve-lès-Avignon
Tel. 90 25 80 06
Fax 90 25 43 57
A 17th-century river mill on the River Rhône, just beyond the Tour Philippe-le-Bel. 20 rooms. Restaurant with dining room which overlooks the river.

Le Prieuré ▮▮▮
place Chapitre,
30400 Villeneuve-lès-Avignon
Tel. 90 25 18 20
Fax 90 25 45 39
In the heart of town is this superb restaurant with park, shaded garden and terrace, as well as a hotel with 26 luxurious rooms.

Aix and Cézanne Country

AIX-EN-PROVENCE

Aix has aged well. It was the first Roman town in Gaul, a citadel and spa founded in 125 BC as *Aquae Sextiae* ('the waters of Sextius'; see p.13). It is one of those blessed towns that win affection without needing the aid of spectacular monuments or richly endowed museums (although these are here also), and which will force a grateful smile out of the most world-weary traveller.

Historically it has enjoyed several great moments: first, under the Romans, then when it became capital of Provence and residence of the counts in the 12th century, and finally under Good King René, from 1471-80, after which it lost out to boisterous Marseille.

There's a good reason why Aix is called 'the Provençal Florence': there is a Florentine mix of aristocratic elegance in the streets. Walking beneath the plane trees or beside the fountains along the **Cours Mirabeau** is always refreshing. One side of the street is lined by gracious, 17th-century mansions, while the other is a bustle of cinemas, boutiques and cafés. This is the place to find *calissons*, the local delicacy made from ground almonds and candied melon. It is also the site of the Café des Deux Garçons; a rendezvous there is one of the few obligations that Provençal life imposes.

The older generation still come to Aix to take the waters (the moss-covered fountain in the middle of the Cours Mirabeau spurts water at the natural temperature of 34°C/93°F), but the university helps keep the spirit of the town young.

Although of interest due to its construction, the cathedral often loses out to its exquisite, Romanesque **Cloître Saint-Sauveur**. Chamber music and choral recitals are held here during the summer music festival, while opera is performed behind the cloister, in the Palais de l'Ancien Archevêché, which also houses a **Tapestry Museum**. More important are **81** the 15 Flemish **tapestries** in the 26 panels of the cathedral's nave and choir. These tell the story of Christ and the Virgin Mary, and were originally designed in 1511 for Canterbury Cathedral, but were bought for Saint-Sauveur in 1656 by one of its canons.

The cathedral also houses a **triptych** by Nicolas Froment, *The Burning Bush* (1465), in which Good King René and Queen Jeanne de Laval kneel on either side of the Virgin Mary, seated in the burning bush and clutching the Infant Jesus. The **baptistery**, some of it 4th-5th century, dates from medieval times.

The **Musée Granet** houses one of Rembrandt's last self-portraits (1665), among a variety of other masterpieces. The French collections contain a special section on Provençal artists including Cézanne, and François Granet, a pre-Impressionist artist from Aix.

Paul Cézanne spent most of his life in Aix, and his studio (Atelier de Cézanne, 9, avenue

Paul-Cézanne), set in the hills outside Aix, has been preserved as a small **museum**, including his palette, cape, beret, and other personal belongings. The best way to evoke his memory is to drive for 14km (9 miles) east of Aix on the D10 to the subject of some of his most famous landscapes – **Montagne Sainte-Victoire**. Despite forest fires in 1989, the sharp angles and jagged shapes which became 'slabs' of colour, and were so instrumental in the development of Cubism, are still as evident as ever.

CÉZANNE CIRCUIT

In Aix itself, there are plenty of Cézanne reminders, such as the trails of paving stones with a little golden C, which indicate the routes the painter used to take to get to his home, studio, church and so on. You can also visit the Rue de l'Opéra,

A typical tree-lined road of the Midi – so pretty, but watch out for some of the drivers!

where he was born in 1839, and the rue Matheron, where he lived with his parents. After that, drive the 60km/38-mile circuit around his 'territory'.

From Aix, head now for **Le Tholonet**, with its 18th-century château, then on to **Puyloubier**, from where courageous hikers climb in about 4 hours to the Priory of Sainte-Victoire (also accessible from Les Cabassols, which is 13km/8 miles from Aix). **Vauvenargues** is best known for its tiny château, which Picasso bought in 1958 and where he lived for the last 20 years of his life. The **Barrage de Bimont** reflects the stunning shapes of Montagne Sainte-Victoire in its peaceful waters.

SALON-DE-PROVENCE

The car was almost the ruin of **Salon-de-Provence**, which used to lie right on the main north-south highway, but the old town has now been largely saved by the arrival of the motorway, which has reduced the traffic load. Not all noise has disappeared though; Salon-de-

83

Provence is the centre for the *Patrouille de France*, the ace pilots' squadron, who hurtle across the sky when you're least expecting it.

Stop next immediately at the **Place Crousillat** (offering welcome shade), linked via the Porte de l'Horloge to Salon's main thoroughfare, the **Rue de l'Horloge**. Within the walls of the mighty **Château de l'Empéri** is the expert **Musée de l'Armée**. The château is one of the biggest and most beautiful in the whole of Provence, with some parts dating as far back as the 12th century.

The famous astrologer and fortune-teller, Michel Nostradamus, lived at Salon, and predicted to within a minute the date and hour of his death on 1 July 1556.

Marseille

Poor Marseille. Unloved by those who don't know it and avoided by those who fear its reputation as the 'Chicago of France'. Even Mme de Sévigné was said to have remarked in 1673: 'The air here has something rascally about it'.

Take time out in ebullient Marseille, an eclectic and lively port that has seen so many arrivals.

This tough, gritty metropolis, cradled by the hills behind its back, is hard to overlook, however. France's oldest city, founded by Greek colonists over 2,500 years ago, it is also the nation's second largest town – though this noisiest and most boisterous of ports is not exactly a prime tourist attraction. It does have immense character, however, and is renowned for its *bouillabaisse*. The Marseillais insist it's the best in France (and it's not wise to argue).

The Marseillais may well be pushy and gabby, but they are full of personality and play the meanest game of *boules*. The politicians make their Chicago counterparts look like choirboys, and endless police raids have still not managed to break the French Connection. With a bit of common sense, however, you (and your wallet) will come out intact, having enjoyed a lively day.

Soak up the atmosphere on the main thoroughfare of the **Canebière** (long known as 'can o' beer'), where sailors from the world over have broken both hearts and noses. You can't miss the mosaic of immigrants who have arrived over the centuries; their origins are apparent everywhere: in shop signs, conversations and faces. Excellent shopping is to be found in the pedestrian streets leading off the Canebière.

The **Vieux Port** marks the spot where Phocaean-Greek merchants from Asia Minor docked to create their western Mediterranean trading post. Unfortunately it's a mere 6m (19ft) deep, so other moorings had to be found for most vessels. Today it is a colourful harbour for yachts and motor launches. From the Quai des Belges, take a cruise out to the **Château d'If**, the island prison which inspired Alexandre Dumas' *Count of Monte Cristo*. It also offers a great view of the harbour and town, putting it all into perspective. **85**

Haute-Provence

Haute-, or Upper, Provence offers many of the scents and savours of Basse-Provence, tinged with a freshness imparted by the altitude. It's rugged and enchanting.

MANOSQUE

Manosque is the gateway. Do not judge it on its outer boulevards, but rather explore the interior. Enter by the 14th-century **Porte Saunerie**, which precedes the Grande-Rue leading to the remodelled Église Saint-Sauveur and the **Place de l'Hôtel-de-Ville**, where the town hall occupies an 18th-century house. Porte Soubeyran has a wrought-iron tower, while all around in the streets and squares life goes on as always (with the exception of changes from the arrival of the nuclear power station nearby).

Jean Giono's works, such as *Regain*, tell you more about the town. He spent his life here and describes it with an affection that was reciprocal: there is a museum devoted to him.

THE LAND OF LAVENDER HONEY

In the sweet-smelling countryside, with truffles and thyme, lavender and honey, Haute-Provence comes into its own.

In this context, the solitude and harshness of the landscape are sometimes forgotten. Take the road to Forcalquier, stopping off in **Reillanne**, with its surprising wall-belltower, and **Mane**, with its lovely houses. **Forcalquier**, in a pretty site on a hill at 550m (1,804ft), had its Golden Age in the Middle Ages, with reputed troubadours and minstrels and plenty of religious activity. The 13th-century **Couvent des Cordeliers** was one of the first in Provence, but suffered in the religious wars at the hands of the Protestants and *routiers*, who were the undoing of the town. Climb up to the old city and the citadel for the **view**, and note the lovely cemetery.

Again for a view, but of a somewhat different sort, head for **Lurs**, down over the Durance and up over the string of fifteen oratories, leading up

300m (984ft) to the chapel of Notre-Dame-de-Vie. Nearby is the **Prieuré de Ganagobie**, a harmonious, 12th-century Romanesque church (1135-73), with fascinating mosaics. The Gregorian chants are extraordinarily moving in the setting.

Another example of early Provençal art is the almost austere, 11th-century **Église de Saint-Donat**, which captures the light in a remarkable way. From here you look down on the 100m (328ft) rocky silhouettes of the **Pénitents des Mées** scattered over 1 mile (1.5km) along the Durance.

Montagne de Lure, a sort of natural prolongation of Mont Ventoux, rises as you approach **Sisteron**. At 1,826m (6,000ft), it provides a spectacular view over the Alps.

Sisteron stands guard like a lookout between the Dauphiné and Provence. For those coming from the north, this is where the olives begin, while for those approaching from the south, it is the start of the Alps. The River Durance slices its way through the wall, separating the two 'worlds', and man has done his level best to complete the job of keeping the

---

Pride of Prudes

Everyone knew that King François I was an inveterate womanizer; his reputation preceded him wherever he went. Consequently, beautiful Honorade de Voland realized what was in store for her as soon as she was designated to give the king the keys of the town on his visit to Manosque in 1516.

She was made of stern stuff though, and rather than fall prey to the seductive charms of the king, she temporarily disfigured herself by exposing her face to sulphur fumes, so managing to avoid the sovereign's attentions.

As a result of this event, Manosque acquired the nickname of 'Manosque the Prudish', an unfitting title for a town situated in the world's capital of *galanterie*.

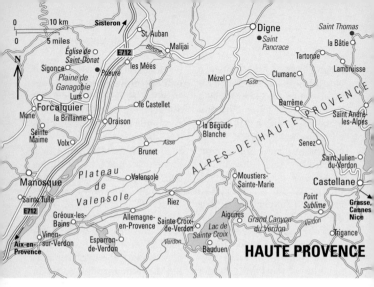

two apart, by building an unassailable citadel on high.

Sisteron's cathedral, **Notre-Dame-des-Pommiers**, mixes Lombard styles and Provençal Romanesque. The old medieval town starts near the cathedral and consists of a maze of streets, tortuous, vaulted alleyways (*andrones*), and staircases. Dominating the scene is the **citadel**, surveyor of many a dramatic event since the 11th century. Today it is used for hosting events in summer.

Not for nothing is **Digne** called Digne-les-Bains – the curative powers of its waters have been used since antiquity. At 600m (1,968ft), it has all the reposing virtues of a spa town. It is also the lavender capital, surrounded by fields of the aromatic plant.

GRAND CANYON DU VERDON

This is Provence's answer to Arizona, perhaps not as big, but the vistas are just as spectacular. Since access was once so difficult, the area remained barely known until recently, and even today has kept something of its aura of mystery. The first modern explorer, the famous geologist E A Martel, came here in 1906 in top hat and cape, travelling in a rickety canoe with just a farm ladder as climbing equipment.

The emerald waters of the River Verdon run 170km (106 miles) through ravines sometimes only 6m (20ft) wide, but 700m (2,300ft) deep. If you want to explore the canyon bottom, ask at the tourist offices of either **Castellane** or Moustiers-Sainte-Marie about guided tours – 4 days on foot, 2 days by canoe, although the latter is especially hazardous for novices because of rocks. To make the most of a visit, ask for suggestions according to the amount available. The GR 4 trails (see p.91) stake out good routes for 6-hour walks.

'Napoleon stopped in Castellane – why don't you?' asks the sign by the road. Starting out from here, the D952 winds along the right bank at the top of the gorge, past well-marked *belvédères* (look-outs), including popular **Point Sublime**, near Rougon, as well as the Mayreste, and the Galetas.

Moustiers-Sainte-Marie is a delightful, colourful village in a dramatic setting beneath precipitous cliffs. Look first at the cross slung on a huge metal chain, 150m (500ft) up between two apparently unconquerable peaks. Placed by a returning Crusader at around 1250, he offered it as thanks to the Lord for his liberation from the Saracens who held him prisoner for two years.

The village's greatest fame comes in the form of its milky white, enamel ceramics. Celebrated for their finesse since the Middle Ages, and covering five distinct periods of production, output came to a stop in 1874, and was only resumed in 1926. The fascinating **Musée de Faience** fills in all the background information, and you could buy some pieces as souvenirs from the Atelier Saint-François (ask for a signature and the authorization *véritable Moustiers*, authenticating it as 'genuine Moustiers').

Riez, nearby, boasts some interesting Roman remains. **89**

What to Do

Provence caters to all tastes. For sports enthusiasts there's sailing, tennis, riding, fishing, mountaineering, deep-sea diving, even skiing.

Shoppers have the choice of markets vivid enough to fire the imagination of artists, and boutiques where standards of design are frequently as high as the price

As for the children, there is no need to worry; the problem is getting them to bed, not keeping their interest. If all else fails, there are plenty of amusement parks and the sea is never far away.

Sports

Not only is the climate ideal for all outdoor sports – and it lasts for most of the year – but the infrastructure is also excellent. Find out from the local tourist office what's going on in the less busy, inland areas, if you want a bit more space away from the crowds.

Cycling

With so many country tracks, Provence is a cyclist's paradise. A VTT (*vélo tous terrains*) mountain bike is not generally necessary, but they are widely available. If you're going cycling, it might be useful to remember the following items: sun-cream, a windjammer, lip cream, glucose tablets, and a map. More than anything though, try to travel light (less than 10kg/22lb), and beware even of the Alpilles foothills!

Riding

For riding, you could scarcely think of a better setting than Eygalières, at the foot of the Alpilles, where the sport has been practised since the 1950s. You can hire a horse for an hour, a day or a week (including instruction) just about anywhere, but the most frequented areas are the Camargue, Ventoux, Alpilles, Gorges du Verdon, and the Vaucluse *département* in general, as well as the mountains and hills above the Côte d'Azur, the

Hills, heat and heavy traffic may be daunting to some cyclists, but the rewards are superb.

Maures, the Esterel, and the Vallon des Merveilles.

For information, try the Association régionale pour le tourisme équestre, 28, place Roger Salengro, 84300 Cavaillon; tel. 90 78 04 49. For general information, contact the Fédération pour Randonneurs équestres de France, 16, rue des Apennins, 75017 Paris; tel. (1) 42 26 23 23.

Hiking

Provence walks range from gentle to sturdy. Most are accessible for three-quarters of the year, although the higher, more demanding ones should be left to the experts in winter. Don't underestimate Provence – people get lost every year.

There are plenty of family-type walks on Mont Ventoux, Montagne de Lure and Montagne de Lubéron. Near Aix and Marseille, try Montagne Sainte-Victoire, the Massif de la Sainte-Beaume, and the *calanques* along the coast round Cassis. Easy-to-see white and red markings indicate that the track is on a GR (*Sentier de Grande Randonnée*) or PR (*Sentier de Petite Randonnée*). These trails are clearly marked, and excellent *Topo-Guides* devoted to each are very helpful (available in local bookshops). Some *sentiers* (trails) are 100km (65 miles), some much longer. **91**

Two regional organizations offer information: Association régionale de développement de la Randonnée en Provence-Alpes-Côtes d'Azur (Rando-sud), Mairie, 04700 Lurs; tel. 92 31 01 47; and the Association départementale des Relais et d'Itinéraires des Alpes-de-Haute-Provence (ADRI), 42, boulevard Victor-Hugo, 04000 Digne; tel. 92 96 05 08.

The latter organizes weekend and theme walks, and both give very useful information on *refuges* (huts), campsites and stops along the way.

Golf

Golf has become very popular in France in the last few years, and there are 18-hole courses throughout the area.

Aix-en-Provence: *Golf de Marseille/Aix*, Domaine Riquetti, 13290 Les Milles; tel. 42 24 20 41; *O'Golf*, chemin des Aubépines, 13090 Aix; tel. 42 59 91 90 (6 holes).

Avignon: *Golf Grand Avignon*, Les Chênes Verts, BP 121, 84270 Vedène; tel. 90 31 49 94.

*T*he balmy Provençal climate has ideal temperatures in which to practise your shots.

Les Baux-de-Provence: *Golf des Baux-de-Provence*, Domaine de Mainville, 13520 Les Baux-de-Provence; tel. 90 54 37 02; *Golf des Servanes*, Domaine des Servanes, 13090 Mouriès; tel. 90 47 59 95.

Salon-de-Provence: *Club de l'École de l'Air*, 13300 Salon-de-Provence; tel. 90 53 90 90 (13 holes).

Deep-Sea Diving

The Comité régional Provence d'Études et Sports sous-marins, 38, av. des Roches, 13007 Marseille; tel. 91 52 55 20 will advise you on deep-sea diving. Without a licence, it is strictly forbidden to carry a gun. Photography and observation are open to all, however, and the flora is beautiful along the coast at a depth of 10m (33ft).

Fishing

Deep-sea fishing is, sadly, not as good as it used to be in the Mediterranean. The *rascasse* (some weighing up to 34 kilos) used in *bouillabaisse*, require enormous patience and skill, and may be out of reach, but there are still enough small fry. The Rhône has good stocks of eel, while trout reach a good size in the upper reaches of the Durance, Verdon, Ouvèze, Vésubie and Tinée. A permit can be obtained from sports shops.

Swimming

Although the Côte d'Azur has cleaned up most of its beaches, its prices are still sometimes inflated. Watch out for the occasional jellyfish (*méduse*). Inland there are plenty of swimming pools (*piscine*), including nine in Aix and six in Avignon. Many rivers also have zones set aside for swimming. Look out too for signs warning *baignade interdite* (swimming forbidden).

Bullfights

Bullfighting continues to be a controversial issue. Nonetheless Spanish experts agree that those in Arles and Nîmes, in the superb settings of the Roman amphitheatres, are highly artistic and professional.

93

Shopping

As well as offering the usual goods found all over France (handicrafts, perfumes, fashion), Provence also has its own specialities, ranging from colourful market stalls to distinctive *banons* cheeses.

Style means everything in France, from a humble wrapper around *pâtisserie* to the design of a tin of olives. There's variety, too: you don't ask for 'bread', but for a *baguette*, *ficelle*, or *pain de campagne*; not 'ham', but *jambon de Bayonne*, *torchon*, *jambon de York*, or *jambon de montagne*. Watch the locals discuss and compare goods – they want the best, and at the right price.

For opening times of shops see p.133.

Where to Shop

The best prices and the biggest choice are found at the *hypermarchés* (hypermarkets) and *supermarchés* (supermarkets) on the outskirts of towns. Markets (see below) are far more fun and more personal. Department stores (*grandes surfaces*) in Marseille, Avignon and Arles are well worth a visit, and the goods available are often far from 'downmarket'. Otherwise, if it's gifts you're looking for, try one of

Don't be under any illusion – but have lots of fun – scouring through 'antiques'.

the local craft shops which advertise in the *syndicat d'initiative* (tourist office); they are concentrated in tourist centres, but sell excellent and creative items. If what you're buying is for a gift, ask for *un emballage cadeau* for the wrapping.

Markets

What could be more inviting than a Provençal market, with its profusion of fresh, exotic and colourful fruit and vegetables? Virtually every town of any size has its own, which has usually been held on the same day for a handful of centuries. Arles and Aix are impressive just for their size and animation, but markets at Apt, Carpentras or Manosque are charming too. In Aix there is a market virtually every day: in Place Richelme for fruit and vegetables every morning, and Place des Prêcheurs on Tuesday, Thursday and Saturday. Carpentras has a *marché aux truffes* (truffles market) every Friday morning between the end of November and beginning of March.

A word of warning: market day means traffic, and parking may be even worse than usual. Also, look around and compare prices and quality like the locals do – there can be some surprising differences, though there is no haggling.

What to Buy

Antiques: *brocantes* (second-hand shops) are all over, and if you're looking for cheer and originality, anything from old-fashioned oil lamps to wine bottles can be found *en masse*. L'Isle-sur-la-Sorgue has a *brocante* fair every year. More serious antique dealers are found in the bigger centres. A visit to a *vente aux enchères* (auction), advertised in the local press, on posters and at the *Hôtel des Ventes* (auction house), provides local colour as well as occasional bargains.

Ceramics: potters of all nationalities have found a good market in Provence, and their wares are often distinctive and highly individual. The attractive, centuries-old pottery of **95**

Moustiers-Sainte-Marie (see p.89) is not overpriced.

Cheese: *banons* (goat cheese wrapped in a chestnut leaf) from the Alps of Haute-Provence are found everywhere, and are light and easy to pack.

Clothes: main towns and certain smaller places (such as Carpentras) have all the chic (and prices) of Paris, and tend to specialize in summer casual and beach wear.

Confectionery (*confiseries*): the sweet-toothed are in for a treat. Each town seems to have a speciality – just look in the window of the top *confiseur* in town to see what it may be. Try *calissons* (sweet almond biscuits) in Aix; *fruits confits* (candied fruit) in Apt; *berlingots* (boiled sweets) in Carpentras; almond biscuits (*caladons*) in Nîmes and *tartarinades* in Tarascon.

Crafts: Provence offers many crafts: pottery, glass-blowing, weaving, jewellery, ceramics, wood and stone sculpture, tapestry, dried leaves, seaweed, and a range of other surprise materials. For such goods, it's best to go direct to the artisans themselves. Among the many villages and towns noted for crafts are: Ménerbes and various towns in the Lubéron; Vénasque; Vachères, near Forcalquier (weaving); and the villages in the Alpilles.

Farm produce: fresh and tasty fruit and vegetables can be bought direct from the producers at roadside stalls.

Herbs: this is obviously the place to buy your *herbes de Provence* (unless you come across them on your walks).

Honey (*miel*): Provence honey is excellent, with the aroma of lavender and rosemary. Some is made by monks at abbeys such as Sénanque (see p.64). It's worth every penny.

Olives: not only are the trees with the silvery-green leaves and tortured trunks picturesque, the wood is also good for ornaments. Table olives, green

96

*T*here are souvenirs to tempt you at every stall – and Provence caters
for all tastes and pockets.

or black, turn any dish into a feast. Everyone has their favourite: ask to try *pitchoulines*, from near Nice or Les Baux. Beware if you buy large jars not to get imported ones (production is not great enough in France and competition from Mediterranean countries of the EC is tough). Olive trees in Nyons (800,000 of them) pro-

duce a variety called *la tanche*, reputedly among the best and not grown elsewhere.

Olive oil (*huile d'olive*): Provence olive oil is a surprising (and pleasant) local speciality, which makes a good present.

Perfume: though you can buy perfumes everywhere, it's still **97**

nice to purchase them in the place of production. At the centre of the industry is Grasse (above Cannes), but there are plenty of perfume producers all over Provence (at Dieulefit/Nyons for instance), not to mention packets of lavender, essences, soaps and other delightful *sent-bon*.

Records: the Abbey of Sénanque (see p.64) offers records of Gregorian chants. Alternatively, Provençal folkmusic with fife and *tambourines* makes an unusual reminder of your stay.

Santons (Christmas crib figures): nothing is more typically Provençal than *santons*, the little ceramic figures which are found in cribs in churches and private houses all over Provence. Sometimes whole towns of *santon* figures, dressed in typical Provençal costume, are exhibited at the side of a road. They are not expensive and are a genuine local product.

Spirits (*eaux de vie*): take back some *pastis* as a reminder of your holiday. For **liqueurs**, Sénanque (see p.64) produces *La Sénancole* and other local tipples. As either a dessert wine or, alternatively, a cooling aperitif, the Muscat-like *Beaumes-de-Venise* (see p.29) or *Rasteau* is delicious.

Wine: Provence offers the perfect opportunity to stock up on *Côtes-du-Rhône* or *Côtes-de-Provence,* straight from the wine-tasting cellar. Most of the wines which are from the Vaucluse, Var and Bouches-

A dilemma – should you choose international perfumes or tempting local Provence ones?

du-Rhône (reds, whites and rosés) regions are good and reasonably priced local vintages, best drunk young, while *Gigondas* and *Châteauneuf-du-Pape* (red wines) (see p.41) are more expensive.

Festivals

All year round Provence brims with fairs and festivals (*terre de fêtes*). Thanks to the region's partially separate development from most of France, local folklore flourished.

Through the *Félibrige* (see p.22), Frédéric Mistral did a lot to help it survive during the last century, and today enthusiastic societies aim to keep traditions going.

The characteristic music of Provence is the pipe and drum. The thin but cheerfully reedy *galoubet* (fife), and the light tap-tap rhythm of the *tambourine* (long drum) instantly raise bucolic images of Provençal shepherds. The accompanying dancing in red, white and black costumes and black hats is full of spirit.

Some towns celebrate specific festivals, such as the *bravade de Colmars* held on the 24 June, which is sadly now disappearing. The *bravades* in Saint-Tropez on 16-18 May celebrate the town's war-torn past, when it had to defend itself against numerous attacks. The much-repaired costumes have been handed down from generation to generation.

In a similar vein, at Les Baux it's the *Fête de Pastrage*; at Castellane the *Fête du Pétardier*; at Tarascon the *Fête de Sainte Marthe* and *Fête de la Tarasque*; and at Valréas the *Fête du Petit Saint Jean*. For most, however, the greatest of them all is at Saintes-Maries-de-la-Mer (see p.57) on 24-25 May, when the gypsies of Europe come together and, in a mixture of religious fervour and showbiz, carry the statue of the Virgin Mary to the sea.

Though the weather in December may not be too clement, a Provençal Christmas in a church such as at Les Baux, with real shepherds and *santon* figures (see p.98), is a uniquely moving experience. **99**

Listed below are the highlights of the annual festivals in Provence; full details can be found in the tourist office booklet *Provence en fête*. Also available is *Provence, Terre de Festivals*, a brochure updated each year. Such is the popularity of summer festivals that there can be difficulties in obtaining seats – advance booking is often necessary.

The contact telephone numbers below for each town or village operate during the festival months, but if you are in Avignon, you can also book tickets there.

Aix-en-Provence. June: *Aix en Musique*; July: *International Dance Festival*. Tel. 42 23 37 81.

Arles. July/August: *Rencontres Internationales de la Photographie* (Photography in all its aspects). Tel. 90 96 76 06. *Festival d'Arles* (Dance and Theatre). Tel. 90 93 90 90.

Avignon. July: *Festival 'Off'* (theatre performances and 'alternative' shows). Tel. 90 76 84 37.

Manosque. December: *Foire des Jeunes Santonniers* (local gathering of the area's *santon* producers). Tel. 92 87 88 89.

*M*erry-go-rounds do their rounds of country villages, where something's always going on.

Marseille. December/January: *Foire aux santons* (local gathering of all the area's *santon* producers); July-August: *Été Marseillais* (Marseille Summer). Tel. 91 90 25 35.

Martigues. July: *Festival Populaire*. Tel. 42 49 39 40.

Orange. July: the *Chorégies d'Orange* (Music). Tel. 90 34 24 24.

Saintes-Maries-de-la-Mer. 24-25 May and end October: *Pèlerinage des Gitans* (Gypsies' Pilgrimage).

Saint-Rémy-de-Provence. *La Fête de la Transhumance* (at Whitsunday). Tel. 90 92 05 22.

Salon-de-Provence. July: *Le festival de Jazz* (Jazz Festival). Tel. 90 56 00 82.

Sisteron. End July-beginning August: *Les Nuits de la Citadelle* (Festival in the citadel). Tel. 92 61 06 00.

Tarascon. July: *Festival d'Expression Provençale* (Occitan festival). Tel. 90 91 03 52. *Fête de la Tarasque*. Tel. 90 91 00 07.

Valréas. July/August: *Nuits musicales et nuits théâtrales de l'Enclave* (Music and Theatre in the Comtat Venaissin). Tel. 90 35 04 71.

Vaison-la-Romaine. *Choralies* (choirs from around the world perform), takes place every three years.

Entertainment

You only have to be present at the *Festival d'Avignon* to see that much of the most exciting nightlife is on the street and along the café terraces. This is true in most towns during summer, when it's too hot to go to bed early (even though it's fun to get up at the crack of dawn for the delightful cool of the morning).

Away from the cafés, there is plenty of nightlife in the discos. Summer, and the 14th July in particular (the 13th is much celebrated, too) brings scores of small *bals populaires*; you don't have to be a **101** great dancer to join in, and all are welcome. Events are usually posted on telegraph poles and walls in advance.

The Côte d'Azur has most of the sophisticated **nightlife**, though Arles, Avignon and Aix all have enough to satisfy most tastes, and there's always Marseille. Discos are increasingly sited outside towns to avoid disturbance.

Children

In Provence, boredom is unlikely to become a problem with children. The sun can be, though, so don't forget to use plenty of protective sun cream. Between the outdoor activities on offer and organized attractions (such as artisans at work – watch *santons* being made, see p.98) as well as the nature parks, there is usually enough to keep even the grumpiest of children happy.

In addition to these attractions, the many **leisure parks** will help to fill in any spare time. Listed below is a selection of the main ones:

102

El Dorado City, *Château-neuf-les-Martigues* (*Bouches-du-Rhône*): a Far West show, Mexican restaurant, shops, and a forest for picnics.

OK Corral, *Cuges-les-Pins* (*Bouches-du-Rhône*): with an authentic Western village offering special shows. Three snack bars and a cafeteria.

Aquacity, *les Pennes-Mira-beau* (*Bouches-du-Rhône*): an aquatic park with 2,500sq m (26,900sq ft) of pools, as well as 400m (1,312ft) of toboggan runs. For mum and dad there are solariums and restaurants.

Parc Minifrance, *on the RN7 route de Nice, at Brig-noles* (*Var*): 'La belle France' in miniature (open until 2am in summer).

Niagara, *on the route de Canadel, la Mole* (*Var*): six giant toboggans, waves, *Ham-mam* (a Turkish steam-bath), bars, shops, and restaurants.

Aqualand, *Saint-Cyr-sur-Mer* (*Var*): six toboggan trails and rapid rivers.

Aquatica, *on the RN98 route at Fréjus* (*Var*): waves, toboggans, a lagoon, and a huge restaurant.

Eating Out

A FEW TIPS

The **menu** for a French meal can consist of anything from a simple three or four courses, to a gargantuan feast of eight or more. If you're daunted by the size of the menu, choose the *à la carte* solution, but you'll be paying more for each item selected.

The word *carte* means 'a menu', while the word *menu* is the suggested meal of the day at a fixed price. This is usually worth considering, as it's well thought out, often regional and usually very good value for money.

Since French meals are virtually a ritual, a certain **etiquette** sometimes surrounds them. Visiting holiday-makers

Outdoor living – paella for all and a spirit of camaraderie – at Vaison-la-Romaine.

*E*ven if you don't feel hungry in the hot weather, it'll be hard to resist the culinary temptations.

need not worry, however, because for them, this tends to relax considerably. Nevertheless, in the grander establishments, wearing jeans, bathing costumes or shorts is generally not appreciated, except beside the pool or beach.

All restaurants are obliged by law to display their prices, including service charges, out-side. Tipping is not obligatory, but if the service has been especially good, an extra 5-10 percent on top of the bill is appropriate. However, it is customary in general to round up the overall bill. Look out for the phrase *service non compris* or *service en sus*, where service is *not* included.

EATING IN FRANCE

French **breakfasts** are traditionally summary affairs, with bread, butter, jam and croissants, and a jug of coffee, pot of tea, or cup of chocolate, the whole being defined by the term 'continental'.

Of late, however, this has changed. Orange juice, corn-flakes, toast and other innova-tions have appeared (even the buffet breakfast), as French youngsters have caught the habit. This has allowed some hoteliers to raise the price of breakfast to almost that of a decent meal.

It's frankly much more fun (not to mention less expen-sive) to go to the local bar for a *petit noir* (a little black coffee) and croissant. You'll watch a town come to life as the locals come in for a quick coffee, glance at a paper and rush off to work. Incidentally, the ma-jority of Frenchmen avoid *café crème* (milk coffee), since it's considered filling and kills the taste of real coffee.

In general, the French are not inclined to **mid-morning snacks**, preferring to wait for lunch, but a small coffee (*ex-press*), is almost *de rigueur*.

Lunch used to be just as important, if not more so, than dinner. Today the trend is to-wards a light, easily digestible lunch without wine. Fast-food outlets, hamburger stalls, *sal-aderies* pizzerias and even *crêperies* flourish, while stan-dard restaurants offer a *plat du jour* (dish of the day) in an effort to attract customers who are anxious to get back to the beach or who are not very hun-gry. Bistros provide sandwich-es a foot long, with often more bread than filling, or plastic-wrapped *croque-monsieurs* at any time (*à toute heure*). Many restaurants nowadays also sug-gest nothing more than a sim-ple salad on a hot summer day – *salade niçoise*, for instance.

Between 12 and 12.30pm you should be able to get a table at a restaurant even if you haven't booked; after that it might get crowded. After 2pm, you run the risk of being refused, though this is becom-ing less common in summer (unless it's totally full up).

If you don't want to be inside on a lovely day, a wise option is to head for a good *charcuterie* or *traiteur*, whose array of cold meats, pâtés, ter-rines, salads, and grated veg-etables, which you can take **105**

*T*he temptations are never-ending – pains au chocolat, chaussons aux pommes, croissants ...

away in plastic containers the size of your choice, will make a delicious picnic. The *charcuteries* in the supermarkets also have a big selection. Be careful, though – before you know it, you can find yourself paying as much for your picnic items as for a full sit-down meal. With this in hand, plus a *baguette*, olives, and a local *Côtes-du-Rhône*, *Bandol* or regional wine (rather than the cheaper but rougher *vin ordinaire*), or even cider, all that remains is to find your spot under a shady tree.

Afternoon tea is not a great French institution. If you're at all demanding, finding a good, strong pot of tea could well prove difficult. For those who can't resist the urge, there are

the *pâtisseries*-cum-tearooms which will usually make more of an effort.

The key to the day, especially after a hot sightseeing programme, is a delicious **dinner**. In summer, this is often served until quite late (9 or 9.30pm in many establishments), but 8 or 8.30pm is usually when most people eat. Knowing where to go can be difficult, simply because there is so much choice. Usually the best plan is just to ask local people ('*Pouvez-vous me re-commander un bon restaurant pas trop cher?*'), since tourist offices hesitate, officially, to recommend one particular establishment over another.

WHAT TO EAT

Although among connoisseurs and gastronomes the cuisine of Provence has plenty of supporters, it isn't considered one of the most refined in France, despite its marvellous selections of fresh fruit and vegetables and unique ingredients found nowhere else – local herbs and olives, for instance.

Olive oil, **herbs** and **garlic** are at the root of this cuisine. The herbs of the Midi go into soups, just as they complement fish and meats. Dried or preserved in oil, the herbs sage, thyme, basil, laurel, fennel, pistou, savory, marjoram, and rosemary enhance flavours and heighten taste. Capers, as well as costly saffron, add to the extraordinary variety available, and also find their way into fish soups and *bourrides*, a somewhat tamer version of the magnificent *bouillabaisse*: white fish served on dry bread, accompanied by a tangy aïoli sauce (a type of mayonnaise sauce with garlic).

Looking for somewhere to enjoy a light lunch? Try a crêpe with plenty of tasty fillings.

Fish

Most big towns have deliveries of fresh **fish** every day except Monday. Though fish is featured on menus throughout Provence, it must be admitted that most of it does not come from the Mediterranean, but the Atlantic or the Channel.

Nonetheless, the **Mediterranean seafood** that Provence does get is mixed with garlic, olives, tomatoes, and the country's most fragrant herbs. For a starter, try the fresh grilled sardines with just a sprinkle of lemon for a taste of the south. *Anchoiade*, a purée of unsalted anchovies in olive oil, makes a delicious hors-d'œuvre on fried bread, as does spicy *tapenade*, a mousse of olives and anchovies, delicious on toast. A *poutrague* is a purée of eggs and fish.

Noblest, and also one of the most expensive of the Mediterranean **fish**, the *loup* (called *bar* elsewhere in France), can be grilled, perhaps with fennel; roasted; stuffed; *meunière* (with butter); or sometimes wrapped in pastry. *Brandade de morue* (cod), sometimes also called *gangasse*, has been adopted by Provence, and is prepared in a special way, served barely warm with croutons. Crayfish *à la provençale*, prepared with fried onions, white wine, and *flambé* tomatoes in cognac, are delicious. Trout (*truite*) is also good, whether it is served *au bleu* (poached), *meunière* (sautéed in butter), or *aux amandes* (sautéed with almonds).

Only in Marseille, you'll be told, can you have the real **bouillabaisse**, that celebrated fish soup, which may contain *rascasse*, John Dory, eel, red mullet, whiting, perch, spiny lobster, crabs and other shellfish. If it doesn't have saffron, it's not authentic, but a lot depends on the chef's whim and the market produce available.

Meat

For your main **meat dish**, expect the meat to be less well done than in most countries. Extra-rare is *bleu*, rare *saignant*, medium *à point*, and well-done *bien cuit* (and quite frowned upon). Steaks (*en-trecôte* or *tournedos*) are often served accompanied by a wine sauce (*marchand de vin*), shallots (*échalotes*), or – a truly rich sin – with bone marrow (*à la moelle*). *À la bordelaise* means with wine sauce, shallots *and* bone marrow.

Provençal chefs excel at *daube de bœuf* (beef stew with tomatoes and olives). Provence, of course, is also the home of frogs' legs (*cuisses de grenouille*), which make a delicious and easily digestible dish when they are bathed in garlic, parsley and butter.

Lamb is also the pride of Provence, particularly *agneau de Sisteron*, with tasty sauces. A roast leg of lamb (*gigot d'agneau*) is served pink (*rose*) unless you specify otherwise. The *charcuterie* you may get will be *le saucisson d'Arles* or mountain ham.

Vegetables and Sauces

Ratatouille, a mixture of the best Provençal vegetables (tomatoes, courgettes, green peppers, eggplants) cooked in oil

and garlic, accompanies many dishes, and is sometimes eaten cold. Or try a *pissaladière*, onion tart with anchovies and black olives, or a *tarte de blettes*, with minced beet leaves mixed with cheese, dried currants and egg.

As to olives, those from Nice, the Vallée des Baux, and Nyons are reputedly the best.

Don't think that everything Italian originated only in Italy. *Ravioli*, Niçois will tell you, began here, as did *gnocchi*, served with a *béchamel* sauce and grated cheese, *au gratin*.

Desserts and Cheeses

Confiseries are quite a speciality. Apart from *calissons* from Aix (see p.81), there are also *fruits confits* (candied fruit) from Apt (see p.64); *nougats* from Sault (or Montélimar) or Sisteron; and *tartes* from Champsaur. *Berlingots* (boiled sweets) are from Carpentras (see p.31); *papalines*, Avignon (see p.38), which also has delicious *melons confits*; *tartarinades*, Tarascon (see p.53); and chocolates, Puyricard, not **109** to mention the lavender and rosemary honeys from just about anywhere in Provence.

While each region favours its specialities, the most famous of the French **cheeses** are widely available: the blue *Roquefort*, soft white-crusted *Camembert*, or *Brie* (the crust of which you can safely remove without offending true connoisseurs), as well as several tasty goat's cheeses (*fromage de chèvre*).

Provence does not produce many of its own cheeses, but you should definitely try a *banon*, goat's or cow's cheese wrapped in a chestnut leaf and tied up with raffia.

WINES AND DRINKS

The whole of Provence seems to be one great wine-growing area, with wines of world class sprouting beside more modest ones which nevertheless turn

*F*ish from the Mediterranean is becoming ever more scarce, but vegetables abound in Provence.

an ordinary picnic into a full-blown celebration.

The vast area of *Côtes-du-Rhône*, which stretches out for 200km (124 miles) along the banks of the Rhône, covers many tastes. They are particularly popular for light *rosés*, which, though scorned by the connoisseurs, are still delightful when drunk cool and make very good picnic wines.

There should always be a **house wine** (*réserve du patron*) at an affordable price, which will be perfectly acceptable, even good. Alternatively,

you will often find that even the less expensive wines come in a carafe, served by the quarter (*quart*) or half (*demi*) litre.

If you don't want wine, or mineral water, state perfectly firmly: '*une carafe d'eau, s'il vous plaît*'. There's no obligation to drink wine or bottled mineral water. However, it's considered sad for the chef if you accompany his exquisite dishes with sweet soft drinks, or tea or coffee, though water is perfectly acceptable.

If you want to order a beer, at least outside on the terrace,

ask for a *demi* or *demi pression* (unless of course you want the whole bottle).

Although statistics consistently rate the French high on the heavy drinker list, the normal Frenchman is less a big drinker, more a choosy one. Increasingly, a half-bottle for two and a glass of mineral water at lunchtime is the rule. Even the young, on the whole, prefer soft drinks or mineral waters which, illogically, are more expensive than their alcoholic counterparts.

Every area of Provence has its own **red wines**. These are usually hearty, enjoyable and full of character – all fine attributes – which is odd, considering that in recent years they have moved from being thought of as the most 'lowly' of standard local wines to very respectable ones. There have been, of course, some very honourable exceptions all along, such as *Châteauneuf-du-Pape* (see p.41) which, along with *Gigondas* (see p.99), are the giants. *Vacqueyras*, *Visan* and *Cairanne* are good and inexpensive in relation to their quality. A good choice for unceremonious meals are the *Coteaux-de-Perrevert*; *Côtes-du-Ventoux*, *Coteaux-de-Lubéron*, and *Coteaux-des-Baux,*

The wines produced round Aix (*Coteaux-d'Aix* or *Palette* – a white wine) are good, too, as are *Bandol* (which ages particularly well) or *Cassis* (also a white) on the coast (both more expensive), and those from the neighbouring *départements* of the Var and Alpes-Maritimes. Many are VDQS (*vin délimité de qualité supérieure*), which is the second highest French wine classification, and means that they contain high-quality wine from an approved regional vineyard.

Don't forget the *vins doux*, such as that from Baumes-de-Venise, a refreshing *Muscat*, or *Le Rasteau*, from vineyards between Orange and Vaison-la-Romaine.

For a change, if you want a different **apéritif**, try a *pastis*, or even a *pastis sans alcool* (alcohol-free). This aniseed-based drink, which suffered a severe drop in interest, is on its way back and belongs intrinsically to the Midi, in the same way as *pétanque/boules* does – and the two often go together. The Midi's younger generation often have a glass of *kir* (white wine with blackcurrant/ *cassis* liqueur).

Finally, though *digestifs* and *alcools* have gone out of fashion (drinking and driving ...), a small *Vieux Marc de Provence*, *Genepy des Alpes* or *Elixir du Révérend Père Gaucher* can sometimes be appropriate. After all, if you're not going to be leaving the hotel ...

Other **drinks** include mineral waters, fruit juice and soft drinks. To avoid too much alcohol in the sun, try a refreshing *citron pressé* or *orange pressée* (fresh lemon/orange). Coffee (unless you specify) will come as a small cup of black coffee. Tea often leaves a lot to be desired.

Châteauneuf-du-Pape-to-be – the embryonic stage of that most noble ecclesiastical wine.

To Help you Order ...

Do you have a table?	**Avez-vous une table?**
Do you have a set-price menu?	**Avez-vous un menu?**
I'd like a/an/some...	**J'aimerais...**
beer	**une bière**
butter	**du beurre**
bread	**du pain**
coffee	**un café**
dessert	**un dessert**
egg	**un œuf**
fish	**du poisson**
glass	**un verre**
ice-cream	**une glace**
lemon	**du citron**
meat	**de la viande**

menu	**la carte**
milk	**du lait**
mineral water	**de l'eau minérale**
potatoes	**des pommes de terre**
salad	**une salade**
soup	**du potage**
sugar	**du sucre**
tea	**du thé**
wine	**du vin**

... and Read the Menu

agneau	lamb	**fruits de mer**	seafood
aïl	garlic	**haricots verts**	French beans
asperges	asparagus	**jambon**	ham
bifteck, bœuf	steak, beef	**langoustine**	prawn
caille	quail	**loup de mer**	sea-bass
calmar	squid	**moules**	mussels
canard	duck	**nouilles**	noodles
chèvre, cabri	goat	**oignons**	onions
chou	cabbage	**poireaux**	leeks
côte, côtelette	chop, cutlet	**pommes**	apples
coquilles	scallops	**porc**	pork
endive	chicory	**poulet**	chicken
épinards	spinach	**riz**	rice
flageolets	green beans	**rognons**	kidneys
foie	liver	**rouget**	red mullet
framboises	raspberries	**thon**	tunny (tuna)

BLUEPRINT
for a
Perfect Trip

An A–Z Summary of Practical Information

> Listed after many entries is the appropriate French translation, usually in the singular, plus a number of phrases that should be of help if you require assistance.

A

ACCOMMODATION (see also CAMPING on p.120, YOUTH HOSTELS on p.140, and the list of RECOMMENDED HOTELS starting on p.66)

In general, good accommodation is not wildly expensive in Provence, when you think what you're getting for your money. Hotels are officially graded by stars, awarded by national or regional official bodies (be careful not to confuse these stars with Michelin recommendations), from five stars for luxury down to one for (sometimes very) basic accommodation.

In mid-summer – which seems to go on for a lot of the year – there can be a severe shortage of rooms. It's advisable either to book in advance, or to reserve a room by lunchtime at latest for the coming evening. At hotels, you are often expected (and asked) to take your evening meal in the establishment, but there is no binding obligation. There is plenty of 'superior' accommodation in first-class hotels, with all the paraphernalia to go with it, especially around the main tourist centres. However, large numbers of middle-bracket hotels, with swimming pools, terraces, and *en suite* facilities at reasonable rates are flourishing, not only in towns, but also in villages, where the settings are lovely and the overall standard of meals excellent.

The *syndicat d'initiative* (SI) or, on general signposts (I) (see p.138), provides lists and will help you find somewhere. In case of emergencies, there are always other solutions which an SI will recommend (particularly easy if you have a car), such as the *ferme-auberge*, *gîte d'étape* and *gîte de randonnée*, *ferme équestre*, and *gîte et meublé*. You won't always make a great saving, however, by going to 'alternative' accommodation.

TYPES OF HOTEL

Relais et Châteaux. These hotels, covering the whole of France, offer several tempting possibilities in the *départements* of Var, Bouches-du-Rhône, the Vaucluse, and Hautes Alpes. All are four- or five-star establishments, some in historical buildings. Their brochure is available from the tourist office (see p.138).

Relais du Silence. A chain of two- to four-star hotels in particularly scenic settings. Some are genuine old stagecoach inns. Establishments are listed in a free booklet published annually and available from the tourist office.

Logis de France. Small or medium sized, family-run restaurant-hotels, mostly in the one- or two-star bracket, almost all of which lie in the villages or countryside outside urban areas. The *Logis de France* put out an annual guide (free if requested from national tourist offices *abroad*). They are classified by a one to three 'chimney' symbol and, though each establishment can be very different, their charter requires a personalized welcome, regional cooking using local produce, and clear-cut, all-inclusive prices. Because they are usually relatively small and very popular, they fill up quickly. Book ahead or get in early.

Hôtellerie familiale. Very similar in intention to the *Logis*, they issue a free annual booklet detailing the amenities of each establishment in their area. The headquarters for the region are: Fédération Régionale des Logis et Auberges de France, Chambre Régionale de Commerce et d'Industrie (CRCI), 8, rue Neuve Saint-Martin, BP 1880, 13222 Marseille; tel. 91 91 92 48.

Table d'hôte/Chambre d'hôte. These are private individuals, generally in the country areas, offering meals and/or bed. For a taste of **117**

'real' France, they are well worth a try. Cooking in private homes is often better than in restaurants, and you'll meet some marvellous people (everyone will eat together). They are signposted at convenient points, or posted on boards outside the house or farm. A *chambre d'hôte* room will include the cost of breakfast.

Gîtes Ruraux. The *Gîtes Ruraux* is an official body with regional offices, which oversees the organization of self-catering holiday accommodation (all-year round) and sets the standards. Accommodation is usually in charming old regional houses, or in renovated farm buildings. Certain minimal standards of comfort (running water, toilets, washing facilities, kitchen facilities) are required. Each *gîte* houses a fixed number of guests, and is rented by the week, but the lease can be prolonged. The price depends on features such as environment, furnishings, and comfort. You can book either by writing, telephoning or faxing the addresses below (*Service des réservations*), or by writing direct to the owners listed on the *white* pages of the complete catalogue, with all conditions obtainable from the same address.

Central Office: Maison des Gîtes de France, 35, rue Godot de Mauroy, 75009 Paris; tel. (1) 47 42 25 43.

Alpes-de-Haute-Provence: Rond-Point du 11 Novembre, 04000 Digne; tel. 92 31 03 14.

Bouches-du-Rhône: Domaine du Vergon, 13370 Mallemort; tel. 90 59 18 05.

Var: 1, boulevard Foch, 83007 Dragignan; tel. 94 67 10 40.

Vaucluse: place Campana BP 147, 84008 Avignon; tel. 90 86 43 42.

Do you have a single/double room for tonight?	**Avez-vous une chambre pour une/deux personnes pour cette nuit?**
with bath/shower/toilet	**avec bain/douche/toilettes**
What's the rate per night?	**Quel est le prix pour une nuit?**

AIRPORTS

The nearest international airport for Provence is Marseille-Marignane (or Nice at the other end), linked by scheduled flights to and from London, Birmingham, Manchester, Newcastle, Glasgow, Edinburgh and Belfast. For information ring 91 91 90 90.

From the airport, coaches (called *cars*, don't get confused) or trains run regularly to Avignon, Arles and Aix-en-Provence, among many other places. Hyères-Toulon and Avignon-Caumont also have regional airports. Air Inter, the French regional airline, serves many cities throughout France, including Paris, many times daily. For inter-city connections, the fast train or TGV (see also TRANSPORT on p.139) is often more practical down the Rhône Valley or along the Côte d'Azur. Nîmes also has an airport which is very convenient for the Comtat Venaissin.

B

BICYCLE and MOPED HIRE (*location de vélos/vélomoteurs*)

Bikes can be hired at the SNCF (National Railways) of some bigger towns, and are advertised all over the place in smaller towns. At some places, ask at the tourist office. Though most bikes rented are in a decent state, check the brakes, lights, etc. You'll need to leave a deposit, which varies considerably. The hire charge is paid on returning the bike, which, for stations, can usually be either at the original point of departure, or at another one in the region (check this first).

Several towns have mopeds or scooters for hire. All moped (and motorcycle) riders and passengers must wear crash helmets. Use of dipped headlights is obligatory at all times of day. Mopeds are not allowed on motorways. Prices can double from one rental shop to the next, so it's worth doing a little shopping around.

I would like to hire a bike, please.	**J'aimerais louer un vélo, s'il vous plaît.**
for half a day/a day/ a week	**pour une demi-journée/ une journée/une semaine**

CAMPING

Camping is, in general, very well organized, with the odd problem in summer due to crowds. Ask for the free catalogue *Camping & Caravanning* from the Office départemental de Tourisme du Vaucluse, 41, cours Jean-Jaurès, 84000 Avignon; tel. 90 82 65 11.

Around 150 campsites are scattered throughout the region, many near bathing areas or *plages amenagées* beside rivers. They vary in size from roughly 30 to 500-600 pitches (*emplacements*). They are clean and most have amenities (showers, swimming pool, bike hire, café/restaurant, tent hire). Early booking in July/August is advisable. Don't camp just anywhere (*camping sauvage*); it's illegal and you could find yourselves forcibly and unpleasantly ejected at some unearthly hour. Look out instead for *camping à la ferme* (which means the farmer is willing to let you camp on his land and use the basic facilities). Also watch for *camping interdit* (camping forbidden).

Have you space for a tent/a caravan?	**Avez-vous de la place pour une tente/une caravane?**
May we camp on your land, please?	**Pouvons-nous camper sur votre terrain, s'il vous plaît?**

CAR HIRE (*location de voitures*) (see also DRIVING on p.123)

Car-hire firms throughout Provence offer French and foreign makes. Local firms sometimes offer lower prices than the international companies, but may not let you return the car elsewhere, at convenient drop-off points. To hire a car, you must have a driving licence (held for at least one year) and a passport. The minimum age varies from 20-23, depending on the firm, or more if an expensive model is involved. A substantial deposit (refundable) is usually required, unless you hold a credit card recognized by the car-hire company. You will also be asked for proof of your hotel or local address. Third party insurance is compulsory. For addresses, look in the telephone book under *Location de voitures*.

I'd like to hire a car today/tomorrow.

Je voudrais louer une voiture aujourd'hui/demain.

for one day/a week

pour une journée/une semaine

CLIMATE

Try to come to Provence in May-June or September-October: not only are there fewer problems with accommodation and crowds, but the climate, the quieter roads and easier parking, not to mention more relaxed hoteliers, definitely make these the best seasons. Even in winter, the temperature rarely sinks below 9-12°C (48-54°F).

		J	F	M	A	M	J	J	A	S	O	N	D
Air	°C	9	9	11	13	17	20	23	22	20	17	12	9
	°F	48	48	52	55	63	68	73	72	68	63	54	48
Sea	°C	13	13	13	15	17	21	24	25	23	20	17	14
	°F	55	55	55	59	63	70	75	77	73	68	63	57

CLOTHING

Although Provence's climate is temperate all year round, even in summer a sweater or jacket can come in handy. The sweltering sun will probably mean you're fine in light sportswear in July and August, but warmer articles can be useful for when the *mistral* wind suddenly appears. For more expensive hotels and restaurants, casual but smart dress is best.

COMPLAINTS

Take inadequacies with tolerance, tact and the awareness that what looks like inefficiency may, in fact, be traditional custom. If you do complain, it is best to remember three things: do it on the spot, calmly, and to the correct person (the *maître d'hotel* or *directeur* in a hotel or restaurant). In extreme cases, a police station (*commissariat de police*) may help, or the regional administration offices (*préfecture* or *sous-préfecture*). If you have reason to complain, then firmness, a sense of humour, and a little French are your most useful assets.

CRIME and THEFT (see also EMERGENCIES on p.127)

The big cities have their share of car thieves, pickpockets and security problems, so watch your valuables, especially in crowds.

Violent crime is rare, but like anywhere else, you should take sensible precautions to avoid problems. Never leave a car unlocked, and if possible, remove the radio and put everything in the boot. Incidents should be reported to the *commissariat de police*. A report will help with insurance.

CUSTOMS (*douane*) and ENTRY FORMALITIES

British visitors need only a passport to enter France, as do nationals of other EC countries and Switzerland. Others should contact the French embassy in their country for entry requirements.

The following chart shows some main items you may take into France and, when returning home, into your own country:

Into:	Cigarettes		Cigars		Tobacco	Liquor		Wine
France [1]	200	or	50	or	250g	1l	and	2l
Australia	200	or	250g	or	250g	1l	or	1l
Canada	200	and	50	and	900g	1.1l	or	1.1l
Eire	200	or	50	or	250g	1l	and	2l
N Zealand	200	or	50	or	250g	1.1l	and	4.5l
S Africa	400	and	50	and	250g	1l	and	2l
UK	400	or	100	or	500g	1l	and	2l
USA	200	and	100	and	2)	1l	or	1l
Within the EC [3]	800	and	200	and	1kg	10l	and	90l

1) For non-European residents or residents outside the EC or from duty-free shops within EC countries.
2) a reasonable quantity
3) Guidelines for non duty-free within the EC. For the import of larger amounts you must be able to prove that the goods are for your own personal use. For EC duty-free allowances see 1) above.

Currency restrictions. There's no limit on the importation or exportation of local or foreign currency, but amounts exceeding 50,000 French francs or the equivalent must be declared on arrival.

I've nothing to declare.	**Je n'ai rien à déclarer.**
It's for my own use.	**C'est pour mon usage personnel.**

D

DISABLED TRAVELLERS

So far, Provence has done little to help the disabled traveller, though this is changing. Regional tourist offices, museums and tour operators are now all making suggestions to help the disabled get around their respective establishments. The most obvious change is simply in people's attitude. Airports are well equipped to assist. The complete guide to facilities for those with handicaps is *Access France*.

DRIVING (see also CAR HIRE on p.120)

To take a car into France, you will need:

- A valid driving licence
- Car registration papers
- Insurance coverage (the green card is no longer obligatory but comprehensive coverage is advisable)
- A red warning triangle
- A set of spare bulbs

Drivers and *all* passengers (back and front) are required *by law* to wear seat belts (where fitted in the back). Children under 10 may not travel in the front (unless the car has no back seat). Driving on a foreign provisional licence is not permitted in France. The minimum driving age is 18.

Driving regulations. Drive on the right, overtake on the left (*serrez à droite* means 'keep to the right'). In built-up areas, give priority to vehicles coming from the right. This *priorité* rule does not apply at **123**

roundabouts (*giratoires*). Outside built-up areas, at such places as junctions marked by signs with a cross or a yellow square on a white background, the more important of two roads has right of way.

Speed limits. When conditions are **dry**, the limit is 130kph (80mph) on toll motorways (expressways); 110kph (70mph) on dual carriageways (divided highways); 90kph (55mph) on other country roads; and 45 or 60 kph (30 or 35 mph) in built-up areas.

Note: when roads are **wet**, all limits are reduced by 10kph (5mph), except for motorways, on which maximum speed in fog, rain or snow is reduced by 20kph (12mph). The word *rappel* in towns and villages reminds you that a speed limit is in force.

Signposting is generally good. Tourist sights are usually highlighted with a brown symbol, making it very easy to distinguish them. A blue road sign directs you to an *autoroute* (motorway), a green one to a *route nationale* (RN – main road), and white to secondary 'D' roads (those maintained by the *département* concerned). For ramblers and hikers, red and white markings at useful points indicate that the path being followed is on a 'GR' (*grandes randonnées*) or 'PR' (*petites randonnées*) trail (see p.91).

Road conditions. Provence is well served with motorways, particularly if you are coming from Paris (the north/south axis). This hasn't exactly helped the landscape, however, and to make it worse, the RNs (main roads) have to bear the brunt of traffic with which they cannot always cope. As some parts of Provence are agricultural, tractors can clog up roads at certain times of the year.

However, driving in France in general, and Provence in particular, is a pleasurable experience, except in the towns, at popular tourist sights, and areas heavily visited in summer (Les Baux or Saint-Rémy). The roads are often less busy at lunchtime, when most people have stopped for a break, and also on Sundays when lorries are not allowed to travel.

On the whole, the French reputation for dangerous driving is grossly exaggerated – but they do occasionally get impatient with **124** foreign holiday-makers. Furthermore, a rather unpopular measure to encourage better driving has been introduced: the driving licence *à points*, whereby bad drivers have points taken off until they have to take their driving test again.

Parking (*stationnement*). This is sometimes impossible in the height of summer, and often difficult the rest of the year. If possible, park outside the town centre and go by foot. Most major tourist sights have parking areas, but towns or villages often have worse problems.

You'll encounter two systems of parking – *zone bleue* (blue zone), and meters. If you want to leave your car in a *zone bleue*, you will need a *disque de stationnement*, a parking disc in the form of a cardboard clock which you can get from a petrol station, newsagent or stationer. Set it to show the time you arrived and it will indicate when you have to leave. Then display it in the car. *Disque obligatoire* means 'disc obligatory'. Meters are often *horodateurs*: you simply place the receipt from the machine in the car window that indicates when you are due to leave. *Stationnement interdit* means 'no parking'. Don't leave your car in a *zone piétonne* (pedestrian precinct), even less if the sign says *stationnement gênant* (parking obstructive). A pictograph shows your car's fate ... being towed away.

Breakdowns (*panne*). There are emergency telephones approximately every 20km (12 miles) on main roads, connected direct to the local police stations which function round the clock. Elsewhere, dial 17, wherever you are, and the police can put you in touch with a garage that will come to your rescue – at a price, of course, so it's wise to take out international breakdown insurance before leaving home. Local garages usually provide towing facilities and spare parts for European cars. Always ask for an estimate before authorizing repairs, and expect to pay hefty value-added tax on top.

Fuel and oil (*essence; huile*). Fuel is available as *super* (98-octane), *normale* (90-octane), *sans plomb* (lead free, 95-octane), *supergreen* (98-octane), and *gas-oil* (diesel). It's customary to give a small tip, particularly if the garage hand checks your tyres. Most fuel stations are self-service, which gets round the problem. On Saturdays, it's worth remembering to fill up, since many garages close on Sundays. **125**

Petrol being quite expensive, it's best not to buy it on motorways; go to supermarkets instead (where it can be up to 15% cheaper).

A tip: Vaucluse car plate numbers all finish with 84, Var 83, and Bouches-du-Rhône 13. It's useful to know if a driver is local or not.

Distance

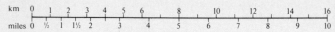

Fluid measures

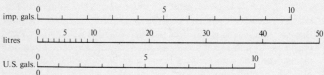

accotements non stabilisés	soft shoulders
chaussée déformée	uneven road surface
déviation	diversion (detour)
péage	toll
priorité à droite	yield to traffic from right
ralentir	slow down
serrez à droite/à gauche	keep right/left
driving licence	**permis de conduire**
car registration papers	**carte grise**
Are we on the right road for ...?	**Sommes-nous sur la route de ...?**
Fill the tank, please.	**Le plein, s'il vous plaît.**
I've broken down.	**Ma voiture est en panne.**
There's been an accident.	**Il y a eu un accident.**

ELECTRIC CURRENT

220-volt, 50-cycle AC is universal. British and American visitors should remember to buy an adaptor.

an adaptor plug/   **une prise de raccordement/**
a battery   **une pile**

EMBASSIES and CONSULATES

The nearest British and US consulates are in Marseille at:

UK: 24, avenue du Prado, Marseille 6^e; tel. 91 53 43 32

USA: 12, boulevard Paul Peytral, Marseille 6^e; tel. 91 54 92 00
Others should get in touch with their representatives in Paris.

Australia (embassy and consulate): 4, rue Jean-Rey, 75015 Paris; tel. (1) 40 59 33 00.

Canada (embassy): 35, avenue Montaigne, 75008 Paris; tel. (1) 47 23 01 01.

Irish Republic (embassy): 12, avenue Foch (entrance on 4, rue Rude), 75016 Paris; tel. (1) 45 00 20 87.

New Zealand (embassy): 7, rue Léonard-de-Vinci, 75116 Paris; tel. (1) 45 00 24 11.

South Africa (consulate): 59, quai d'Orsay, 75007 Paris; tel. (1) 45 55 92 37.

EMERGENCIES (*urgence*)

Dial **17** for the police, and **18** for the fire brigade (*pompiers*), who also answer medical emergencies. For ambulances, call the number in the telephone box.

Police!   **Police!**

Fire!   **Au feu!**

Help!   **Au secours!**

GETTING AROUND (see also AIRPORTS on p.119)

By coach. Daily departures from Victoria Coach Station, London to Marseille and Avignon, where you can change coaches to reach other main towns. Although the trip is long, much of it is overnight and it's an economical way of getting to Provence.

By car. To get there quickly, take the A26 motorway outside Calais. This takes you to Paris, which you circumvent and take the A7, the so-called '*Autoroute du Soleil*', to Lyon and Marseille. Note that the toll (*péage*) is expensive. You may prefer to tackle the latter part of the route on the roads parallel to the motorway.

By train. From Paris, the TGV runs to Marseille (5 hours), via Lyon and Avignon, but it is expensive with its supplement. Anyone living permanently outside France can buy the France-Pass (called France Railpass overseas), which gives unlimited travel for any 4 days within 15 days, or any 9 or 16 days within a month.

GUIDES and TOURS

Further interest is usually added if you visit sights with a knowledgeable and helpful guide. Often at châteaux, and the Palais des Papes in Avignon for instance, they are 'imposed', but so much of the pleasure of Provence is wandering at will.

Try also the SNCF (French National Railways) day trips from Arles (at 24, boulevard Clémenceau; tel. 90 49 36 90) which do the Massif de la Montagnette, the Lubéron, the 'traditional' Camargue and a Van Gogh tour (including Les Baux and Saint-Rémy).

We'd like an English-speaking guide.

Nous aimerions un guide parlant anglais.

LANGUAGE

The French are proud of their language, and handle it with skill and wit. Inevitably, a foreigner will manhandle it, but that's far better, as far as the French are concerned, than not making an effort at all, at least to say the odd phrase (see the front inside cover of this guide).

Never, at all costs, take an understanding of English for granted; if it's not ridiculously excessive, congratulate the person who does speak it – a little encouragement will make them better disposed to help you. In hotels, restaurants, campsites and *syndicats d'initiative*, there will usually be someone who can speak some English.

The French spoken in Marseille and Provence has the warm, rich intonations of the Midi, with a 'twang'. French people from other regions love it, for its associations with fun, sun, and the south in general. It is, however, for those with school French, an added obstacle to comprehension.

LAUNDRY and DRY CLEANING
(blanchisserie; teinturerie, nettoyage à sec)

As a rule, apart from in major centres such as Aix, there are not many launderettes (*laveries automatiques*), and cleaning clothes means a cleaners (*blanchisserie*) or dry cleaners (*pressing*). The bigger hotels will take care of the problem for you, or look in the *Pages Jaunes* of the telephone book under the headings above.

LOST PROPERTY (*objets trouvés*)

In Provence, what goes astray has a good chance of getting back to its owner. On the whole, restaurant and café personnel are very honest about keeping forgotten or lost objects until the owner reclaims them – or in the case of wallets, they will turn them over to the police. If you lose anything, check first at the hotel desk, then at the *commissariat de police* or *gendarmerie*.

I've lost my child/wallet/ handbag/passport.

J'ai perdu mon enfant/ portefeuille/sac/passeport.

MEDICAL CARE (see also EMERGENCIES on p.127)

Before you leave, make sure your health insurance policy covers illness or accident while on holiday. If not, ask your insurance representative, motoring association or travel agent about special holiday insurance plans. Visitors from EC countries with corresponding health insurance facilities are entitled to medical and hospital treatment under the French social security system. Before leaving home, ensure that you are eligible and have the appropriate forms. Doctors who belong to the French social security system (*médecins conventionnés*) charge the minimum.

If you're taken ill or have toothache, your hotel receptionist can probably recommend an English-speaking doctor or dentist; otherwise, ask at the *syndicat d'initiative*, or in an emergency, the *gendarmerie*. Chemists (*pharmacies*) display green crosses. Staff are helpful in dealing with minor ailments and can recommend a nurse (*infirmière*) if you need injections or other care.

In towns throughout Provence, there will be a chemist on duty at night on a rota system (*service de garde*). The name and address of the duty chemist is displayed in the window of other pharmacies. Otherwise, you can get it from the *gendarmerie* or the local newspapers. *Le Provençal* lists chemists and doctors on call (*pharmaciens/médecins de garde*).

MONEY MATTERS

Currency (see also CUSTOMS AND ENTRY FORMALITIES on p.122). The French *franc* (abbreviated F or FF) is divided into 100 *centimes* (ct). Coins come in 5, 10, 20, 50ct; 1, 2, 5, 10, 20F. Banknotes come in 20, 50, 100, 200, 500F.

Banks and currency exchange (see also OPENING HOURS on p.133). Local tourist offices may change money outside banking hours at the official bank rate. Take your passport when you go to change money or travellers' cheques. Your hotel may also come to the rescue, although you'll get a less favourable rate of exchange.

Credit cards are accepted in an increasing number of hotels, restaurants, shops and service stations, as well as being used for obtaining money from cash dispensers (*distributeurs automatiques*). Cards affiliated with the *Carte Bleue* system have the best chance of being accepted.

Travellers' cheques and Eurocheques are widely accepted in France. Outside the main towns, it's preferable to have some cash with you, especially for paying for petrol.

Sales tax. A value-added tax (TVA) is imposed on almost all goods and services. In hotels and restaurants, this is accompanied by a service charge. Visitors from non-EC countries will be refunded the TVA on more expensive purchases. Ask the sales assistant for the necessary form, which has to be filled out and handed to French customs on departure.

Where's the nearest bank/ currency exchange office?	**Où se trouve la banque/le bureau de change la/le plus proche?**
I want to change some pounds/dollars.	**Je voudrais changer des livres sterling/des dollars.**
Do you accept travellers' cheques/this credit card?	**Acceptez-vous les chèques de voyage/cette carte de crédit?**

PLANNING YOUR BUDGET

The following list will give you an idea of what to expect of prices in Provence, but since they vary considerably and rise inexorably, they must be considered approximate. Unfortunately, although the government does what it can to prevent it, prices seem to shoot up unreasonably in the summer season in certain establishments. Also, beware of the accumulated cost of drinks in the course of a day – they can mount up very quickly!

Bicycle/Moped Hire. Mountain bike half day 75F, whole day 100F, week 515F; normal bicycle (*vélo de randonnée*) 50F half day, 70F whole day, 310F a week. Returnable deposit around 500F. Scooter 200F whole day, 840F a week.

Campsite. 2-star site: 2 adults, 2 children over 7 years (under 7s or 5s usually free), car/caravan, electricity, local tax 50-65F.

Car hire. *Peugeot 309* 268F a day plus 3.88F per km, or 3,160F per week with unlimited mileage; *Renault 21* 365F a day plus 4.85F per km, or 4,440F a week with unlimited mileage.

Entertainment, culture. Cinema 35F; discothèque 80-100F (drink sometimes included); festival concert 100-170F; sound-and-light show 80-115F; guided visits 20F (students 11F); Leisure park 45-75F (general entry); helicopter ride (30 mins) 600F per person.

Food and Drink. Bread (*baguette*) 4F, butter 8-14F, olives (100g) 6-8F, *pâté de campagne* (100g) 5-10F, bottle of ordinary wine 12F, bottle of *Gigondas* 30-35F.

Hotels (double room) 2-star 280-400F, 3-star 300-500F, 4-star 400F and up; *chambre d'hôtes* 150-250F.

Meals. Breakfast 25-50F; lunch or dinner (3-5 course *menu*, without wine for two), medium establishment 85-250F; luxury establishment 250-450F; dish of the day 65-85F; bottle of local *Côtes-du-Rhône* wine 70-90F; ½l *pichet* 40F; mineral water 15-20F; coffee 6-14F.

Museums. Around 20-45F (guide 3-5F tip per person *expected*).

Sports activities. Canoe hire (3-4 hours) 60-100F per person (children 40-80 F), includes mini-bus return to departure point; 2 days 180F, one week 450F (kayak slightly more). Horse-riding 70F 1-hour lesson, 600F 10-hour excursion, week 2,700F. Horse and carriage 200F per day per person (with driver). Accompanied walks half-day 50F, full day 70F per person. Pedalo hire 10 F per half-hour.

Telephones: *Télécarte* 50 units 40F; 120 units 96F.

NEWSPAPERS and MAGAZINES (*journaux; magazines*)

During the tourist season, you can be almost certain of getting major British and other European newspapers and news magazines on publication day or, at the very latest, the following morning. The Paris edition of the *International Herald Tribune* is available at all newsagents in resorts and larger towns. Local English-language publications abound. In summer, the local daily, *Le Provençal*, has a small English section on activities for that day in Provence.

OPENING HOURS (*heures d'ouverture*)

Banks are usually open from 9am-5pm on weekdays (many close from 12-2pm) and close either on Saturday (main towns) or Monday. All banks close on major national or regional holidays, and most close early on the day preceding a public holiday.

Main post offices are open 8am-7pm weekdays, 8am-noon Saturday. Post offices in smaller towns usually close for lunch from 12-2 or 2.30pm, and for the day at 5 or 6pm.

Groceries, **bakeries**, **food shops** are open 7am-7pm Monday-Saturday (sometimes later in summer). Food shops and some supermarkets are often open on Sunday morning. Small shops close at lunch from 12.30-2pm or later.

Other shops are open generally 9 or 9.30am-6.30 or 7pm Tuesday to Saturday, closing Monday morning or all day Monday.

Museums, **châteaux**, **monuments** are open from around 10am-5.30pm. Closing day is usually Tuesday, but check first, it frequently changes. During low season, many close or have reduced hours.

P

POLICE (see also EMERGENCIES on p.127)

In cities and larger towns, you'll see the blue-uniformed *police municipale*; they are the local police force, who direct traffic, keep order and investigate crime.

Outside the main towns are the *gendarmes*, who wear blue trousers and black jackets with white belts, and are responsible for traffic and crime investigation. They are usually pleasant, helpful and efficient, but not many speak English.

POST OFFICES

Post offices display a sign with a stylized bluebird and/or the words *Postes et Télécommunications*, P&T, or *La Poste*. (For hours, see p.133.) In addition to normal mail service, you can make local or long-distance telephone calls, buy *télécartes* (phone-cards), and receive or send money at any post office.

Note: While you can theoretically always buy stamps (*timbres*) at tobacconists (*tabacs* displaying a red cone outside), and occasionally at hotels or from postcard or souvenir vendors, the sales people are usually unaware of the correct cost of postage, and can be distinctly disinclined to sell stamps unless you purchase postcards also.

Poste restante (general delivery). If you don't know ahead of time where you'll be staying, you can have your mail addressed to you in any town c/o *Poste restante, Poste centrale*. You can collect it for a small fee on presentation of your passport. If you're British, and are expecting a letter and none arrives, try asking the counter clerk to look under 'E' for Esquire (it's happened more often than you would imagine). Post can be sluggish in the summer months.

express (special delivery)	**par exprès**
airmail	**par avion**
registered	**en recommandé**
134 Have you any mail for ...?	**Avez-vous du courrier pour ...?**

PUBLIC HOLIDAYS (*jours fériés*)

These are France's national holidays. If one of them falls on a Tuesday or Thursday, many French people take the Monday or Friday off as well to make it a long weekend.

January 1	*Jour de l'An*	New Year's Day
May 1	*Fête du Travail*	Labour Day
May 8	*Fête de la Victoire (1945)*	Victory Day
July 14	*Fête nationale*	Bastille Day
August 15	*Assomption*	Assumption
November 1	*Toussaint*	All Saints' Day
November 11	*Armistice*	Armistice Day (1918)
December 25	*Noël*	Christmas Day
Moveable dates	*Lundi de Pâques*	Easter Monday
	Ascension	Ascension
	Lundi de Pentecôte	Whit Monday

In France, school holidays vary from region to region, but as elsewhere, resorts tend to fill up in the summer. In general, children's summer holidays begin in late June and go on to early September. August can be appallingly crowded in big centres.

Are you open tomorrow?   **Est-ce que vous ouvrez demain?**

R

RADIO and TV (*radio; télévision*)

There are three main television channels in France, plus the cable channel Canal Plus. All programmes (except for a few late films) are in French, either made in France or dubbed. You can easily tune in to BBC programmes on either short- or medium-wave radios. In summer Radio 104FM transmits in English all day, and other frequencies have news broadcasts and information in English. You'll be surprised to hear English and American pop music much of the day, interspersed with French of course.

RELIGION

Although France is a predominantly Roman Catholic country, gone are the days when attendance at mass on a Sunday was the rule, not the exception. However, in Provence some traditional respect remains, and ceremonies, especially at Christmas, can be very moving. Jewish synagogues are at Cavaillon, Carpentras, Aix, Avignon and Marseille. Protestants are well represented at Nîmes and Roussillon, but churches are also found in Avignon, Arles and all the major towns (especially in the Côte d'Azur beach towns).

TELEPHONES (*téléphone*)

Long-distance and international calls can be made from any telephone box, but if you need assistance in placing the call, you may be happier doing so from the post office or your hotel (where you'll pay more). In fact, though, the public system is both simple and efficient; the only problem is that more and more phone boxes (virtually all in the big towns and cities and a good number outside) only take *télécartes* for 50 or 120 units (from post offices or tobacconists). Coin-operated telephones guzzle up 50ct, 1F, 2F and 5F coins, so you need a good stock to use this type of phone. To make an international call, dial 19 and wait for a continuous burring tone before dialling the rest of the number. Codes for the main English-speaking countries are:

Australia: 19 61	South Africa: 19 27
Canada: 19 1	United Kingdom: 19 44
Irish Republic: 19 35	United States: 19 1
New Zealand: 19 64	

If you require international enquiries, insert 33 12 between the 19 and the code of the country you want to dial; eg 19 33 12 44 (for the UK). For the US or Canada, dial 11 instead of 1 (19 33 12 11).

For long-distance calls within France there are no area codes (just dial the 8-digit number of the person you want to call), except when telephoning from the provinces to Paris or the Ile-de-France (dial 16, wait for the dialling tone, then dial 1 followed by the 8-digit number). If all else fails, call the operator for help (12).

Minitel: the Minitel has invaded most French homes and public buildings and is on its way to becoming indispensable. It can be used for everything from booking a seat on a TGV train or a theatre ticket to looking up someone's telephone number or address. The Minitel most tourists are likely to meet will either be in their hotel room or at the post office. A useful brochure, *Passeport Tourisme Minitel*, with operating instructions in English is available from tourist offices.

TIME DIFFERENCES

France keeps to Central European Time (GMT+1). Summer time (GMT+2) comes into force from late March to end September. The following chart gives summer time differences.

New York	London	**France**	Sydney	Auckland
6am	11am	**noon**	8pm	10pm

TIPPING

A little tip can go a long way in Provence, all the more so now that in general the tip has been incorporated into restaurant prices. More and more (*except* for museum and château guides, who rely on it) you only give a tip for a particularly appreciated service.

Hotel porter, per bag	4-5F
Hotel maid, per week	50-100F
Lavatory attendant	2F
Waiter	5-10% (optional)
Taxi driver	10-15%
Hairdresser/barber	15% (gen incl)
Tour guide	10%

TOILETS

Regular visitors to France will notice that remarkable progress has been made in recent years. Toilets are now, for the most part, modern, fully equipped, and have wash basins and soap. If you use those in a café, you should at least buy a coffee (or a postcard, if it's also a tobacconists). On beaches, however, they are not always too clean.

TOURIST INFORMATION OFFICES *(syndicat d'initiative)*

Once you arrive, head for the local tourist office – the *syndicat d'initiative* (SI) or *office de tourisme* – usually situated close to the centre of any town or at the railway station. Either may be signposted by the internationally recognized form of **I** (Information). Generally, the *syndicat d'initiative* in smaller towns gives information on more local places of interest, while the bigger *office de tourisme* will provide details on the whole region, and can book accommodation and change foreign currency. Tourist office staff usually go to great pains to help visitors with up-to-date information on prices, transport and attractions. They don't recommend restaurants – at least, not officially. Hours vary, but in the summer most tourist offices open every day except Sunday from 9 or 9.30am-12 or 1pm, and from 1 or 2pm-6 or 6.30pm. (Out of season, hours are limited and many close.) There are French National Tourist Offices in the following countries:

Australia: Kindersley House, 33 Bligh Street, Sydney, NSW 2000; tel. (2) 231-5244.

Canada: 1981 Avenue McGill College, Suite 490, Esso Tower, Montreal, Quebec H3A 2W9; tel. (514) 288-4264; and 1, Dundas Street West, Suite 2405, Box 8, Toronto, Ontario M5G 1Z3; tel. (416) 593-4717.

South Africa: Carlton Centre, 10th Floor, PO Box 1081, Johannesburg 2000; tel. (11) 331 9252.

United Kingdom: 178 Piccadilly, London, England WlV 0AL; tel. (071) 493-6594.

USA: 610 Fifth Avenue, New York, NY 10020; tel. (212) 757-1125; 645 North Michigan Avenue, Suite 630, Chicago, Illinois 60611; tel.

(312) 337-6301; 9401 Wilshire Boulevard, Beverly Hills, California 90212; tel. (213) 272-2661; 1 Hallidie Plaza, San Francisco, California 94102; tel. (415) 986-4174.

Two useful addresses in **Provence** are: Office de Tourisme, 4 Cambière 13001 Marseille; tel. 91 54 91 11, and Office départemental de tourisme et Accueil de France, 41 cours Jean-Jaurès, 84000 Avignon; tel. 90 82 65 11.

TRANSPORT (see also AIRPORTS on p.119)

Buses. Visitors will only really need to use the bus service to visit Cézanne's studio at Aix (see p.82) and the Alyscamps at Arles (see p.52), since the parts of Avignon, Arles or Aix to be visited are all in the centre within easy walking distance. Tourist information offices will have all the details and timetables.

Coaches. The *car* (coach) services are well worth investigating for local travel. All the major towns have a *gare routière* (coach station), and for getting around the countryside, price, comfort and convenience can hardly be bettered. Since much of Haute-Provence is hilly, it's a real pleasure to leave the driver the problems and to take in the scents and sights. Coaches are not always air-conditioned, but in the holiday mood it hardly matters. Contact the tourist information office for details of routes and timetables.

Taxis. In general Provence's taxis are not expensive compared to most European rates, but you'll find that distances within towns are not great and the need for taxis therefore not pressing.

Trains. The SNCF (French National Railways) operate a widespread, comfortable, fast and punctual service. In summer there are over 6 trains a day from Paris to Avignon. The Nice–Digne-les-Bains tour is a very pleasant train journey. There are various types of ticket: *billet séjour*, *billet de famille*, *France vacances*, etc – ask at the tourist office or station before buying a ticket.

139

WATER (*eau*)

Tap water is safe throughout the country, except when marked *eau non potable* (not safe for drinking). Mineral water is also available.

a bottle of mineral water | **une bouteille d'eau minérale**

fizzy/still | **gazeuse/non gazeuse**

WEIGHTS and MEASURES (See also p.126)

Temperature

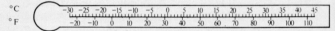

Length

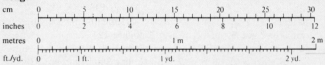

YOUTH HOSTELS (*auberge de jeunesse*)

The Union Régionale des Auberges de Jeunesse PACA (Villa Les Ormeaux, avenue de la Garde, 05200 Embrun; tel. 92 43 32 91) is the regional authority for youth hostels (local offices at Toulon, Avignon, Embrun, and Mallemort). Most hostels offer standard amenities, but none are big, so check in advance. Ask for the free guide to French youth hostels from the Fédération Unie des Auberges de Jeunesse (FUAJ), 27, rue Pagol, 75018 Paris; tel. (16) (1) 46 07 00 01.

Index

Where more than one page reference is given, the one in **bold** is the main entry listed.

141

Berlitz – pack the world in your pocket!

* in preparation